The Young People's History of America's Wars

THE COLONIAL WARS

Prelude to the American Revolution

Illustrated
by
Robert F. McCullough

DON LAWSON

The
struggle between
France
and Great Britain
for supremacy
in North America:
1689–1763

Abelard-Schuman
New York
London

Library of Congress Cataloging in Publication Data

Lawson, Don.
  The colonial wars, prelude to the American Revolution.

  SUMMARY: *Discusses four major colonial wars in North America and the way their outcomes contributed to the causes of the Revolutionary War. Included are King William's War, Queen Anne's War, King George's War, and the French and Indian War.*
  1. United States—History—Colonial period—Juvenile literature. [1. United States—History—Colonial period] I. McCullough, Robert F., 1929–   illus. II. Title.
  E188.L37   973.2   73–38424
  ISBN 0–200–71885–1

NEW YORK
Abelard-Schuman
Limited
257 Park Ave. S.
10010

LONDON
Abelard-Schuman
Limited
158 Buckingham Palace Road SW1
and
24 Market Square, Aylesbury

An Intext *Publisher*

Published on the same day in Canada by Longman Canada Limited
Printed in the United States of America
Designed by the Etheredges

*To
my wife,
Beatrice,
without whom
this work
would not have
been
written.*

Contents

9

PART II

Timeline

1492—   *Columbus rediscovers America.*

1497—   *John Cabot reaches mainland of North America; establishes English claims to continent.*

1513—   *Spanish explorer Juan Ponce de León discovers Florida.*

1524—   *Giovanni da Verrazano explores eastern coastline of North America for France.*

1534–1541   *Jacques Cartier discovers St. Lawrence River, founds Montreal, and opens Canada to French settlement.*

1565—   *Spanish settle St. Augustine; oldest permanent settlement in continental United States.*

1585—	*English make first attempt to establish a colony at Roanoke, Virginia.*
1588—	*English defeat Spanish Armada.*
1607—	*Settlement of Jamestown, Virginia; first permanent English colony in America.*
1608—	*Samuel de Champlain founds Quebec; first permanent French colony in America.*
1620—	*Pilgrims found Plymouth, Massachusetts.*
1622—	*Opechancanough's uprising in Virginia.*
1637—	*Pequot Indian War.*
1644—	*Opechancanough's second—and last—uprising.*
1672—	*Count Louis de Frontenac named governor of Canada.*
1673—	*French explorers Jacques Marquette and Louis Joliet explore upper Mississippi River area.*
1675–1676	*King Philip's War in New England.*
1682—	*French explorer René Robert de La Salle travels length of Mississippi River.*
1689–1697	*King William's War.*
1702–1713	*Queen Anne's War.*
1718—	*French found New Orleans.*
1739–1741	*War of Jenkins's Ear.*
1744–1748	*King George's War.*
1754–1763	*French and Indian War.*
1763—	*Pontiac's Conspiracy*
1775—	*American Revolution begins.*

Part I

One

*The
Lost Colony
of
Roanoke*

On a hot, humid mid-August afternoon in the year 1591, several large English sailing ships dropped their anchors a few hundred yards from Roanoke Island just off the coast of what is today North Carolina. The ships' masters would have preferred anchoring in a more sheltered spot because of the frequent hurricanes in this area, but Roanoke Island had no suitable harbor.

Soon a number of small boats were lowered over the sides of the anchored ships, and oarsmen began the laborious task of rowing through the strong surf toward shore. Standing in the bow of the lead boat and anxiously scanning the island for signs of life was John White.

White was governor of Roanoke Island—the first English colony in America.

The colony had been founded in 1585 and resettled in 1587. Almost completely dependent on England for food and other supplies, the settlement had not prospered. Finally Governor White had been forced to return to England for aid. There he had been delayed for many, many months. Now he feared that his return to Roanoke with the desperately needed supplies might be too late to save the starving colonists.

Governor White's fears proved well-founded.

No sooner were he and the ships' crews ashore than they realized that some strange disaster must have struck the colony in the governor's absence. There was no one there to greet them. Nor were there any bodies or graves. There were, however, certain signs of human habitation left behind by the colonists when they had mysteriously disappeared from the island.

There were the crumbling remains of houses and a half-ruined fortress that had been abandoned so long that tall grass now grew inside its walls. Half-hidden by the grass were several pieces of broken armor. Outside the fort, five chests had been buried and then, apparently dug up and most of their contents destroyed. In one of these chests White recognized the remains of some of his own personal possessions —books, maps and paintings.

But most puzzling of all was the discovery of a large tree from whose trunk the bark had been stripped.

Carved on the stripped tree trunk, in large capital letters, was the single word:

CROATOAN

As White and his party studied the mysterious letters, a strange silence fell over the group. The only sound to be heard was from a soft, late-afternoon breeze that had suddenly sprung up and now sighed through the tall pine and cedar trees. White was aware, even without a word being spoken, how eager the crews were to return to the safety of their ships anchored offshore.

White himself felt a moment's chill, but unlike the others, he did not want to flee this place. He had left members of his family here on Roanoke Island when he had gone to England. He was determined to find out what had happened to them as well as to the other settlers.

The man responsible for the first attempts to establish an English colony in America was Walter Raleigh, famous soldier, writer and favorite courtier of England's Queen Elizabeth. In fact Raleigh was such a great favorite of the queen that although she gave him permission to plant colonies in the New World, she would not let him leave England to take part in the colonizing efforts.

Financed by Raleigh, an exploratory expedition set out in 1584 to find a suitable site for a colony. The site chosen was Roanoke Island (Roanoke came from a similar Indian word), but before returning to England two months were spent exploring the neighboring area. The expedition brought back glowing reports of the richness of the soil and the great abundance of game. It also brought back two Indians, Wanchese and Manteo, who were introduced to Queen Elizabeth as examples of the "gentle, handsome and goodly people" who already lived in America.

The queen was greatly pleased with the success of this first expedition. Raleigh was knighted and the new land was given the name, "Virginia," in honor of Elizabeth who was called, "The Virgin Queen." Actually much of the eastern part of America that was originally called Virginia is now North Carolina.

Sir Ralph Lane was the governor of the first colony sent to Roanoke Island by Raleigh in 1585. John White was also one of the important members of this first group of English settlers. During the next year, he painted numerous pictures of Indian ceremonies. Many of White's paintings still exist and are in the British Museum.

From the beginning the colony fared badly. A fortress and several homes were built, but the settlers made no attempt to grow their own crops. Instead, they depended upon the food and supplies that they had brought with them from home or tried to obtain food from the Indians. Since the Indians depended upon the crops they grew and the game they killed for their own needs, hostility soon developed between the settlers and the Indians. Governor Lane also made enemies of some of the local Indians when he ordered their fields of corn destroyed to punish them for stealing from the colonists. By 1586 the colony faced starvation.

19

At this point, Sir Francis Drake and his fleet of twenty-three warships arrived at Roanoke. Drake had been attacking Spanish shipping in the West Indies and raiding St. Augustine in Florida and other Spanish settlements farther south. He offered to take the Roanoke colonists back to England or to leave them a ship filled with supplies. Governor Lane accepted Drake's offer of the supply ship, but before Drake could put provisions aboard it a hurricane struck the coast and, to save their ships, several masters ordered their vessels to put to sea. Among them was the *Francis*, which had been selected for the use of the colony.

When the hurricane blew itself out, Drake offered the colonists another ship, but by now Governor Lane was thoroughly discouraged and asked Drake to give the colonists passage back to England.

The colonists did not return home empty-handed. With them they brought the potato and tobacco plants, which were widely publicized by Raleigh. Both became popular in England and Ireland. The potato became especially popular in Ireland, where Raleigh introduced it by growing a crop on his estate there. Indian corn, or maize, was also made known to the English by the returning colonists.

But Raleigh was not content with planting potatoes in Ireland. He was stubbornly determined to "plant the English nation in America." In the spring of 1587 he sent out a second group of colonists with John White as governor. The group numbered between 120 and 150 settlers. In addition to the men of the company, there were some seventeen women and nine children.

When the new colony landed on Roanoke Island, White put everyone to work rebuilding the fort and repairing the old houses and building new ones. For a time it appeared that the colony might prosper.

Manteo, one of the Indians who had been taken to England some years earlier, returned with Governor White's party, and was a great help to the colonists in dealing with neighboring tribes. Manteo was baptised in the summer of 1587, the first Protestant to be baptised in America. On August 18 of the same year, Governor White's granddaughter, Ellinor, who was the wife of Ananias Dare, gave birth to a daughter—the first English child to be born in the New World. The baby was christened Virginia Dare.

Unfortunately, it was not long before supplies once again began to run low, and Governor White was requested by the colonists to return to England for aid in one of the ships that had brought them to the island. At first he refused to go, but the settlers were insistent and he finally consented.

When White arrived home, England was at war with Spain, and the country was threatened by invasion. He found Sir Walter Raleigh, Sir Francis Drake and Queen Elizabeth completely occupied with making plans for the impending sea fight between the men-of-war of the English navy and the Spanish Armada. Not a single ship could be spared to send supplies to the struggling Roanoke settlers.

The English navy defeated the Spanish Armada in the English Channel in the late summer of 1588, but the war dragged on for many months after that and English merchant ships were not allowed to sail to America. It was not until 1591 that, with Raleigh's aid, White could obtain the three supply ships that took him back to Roanoke Island—the island which he now found mysteriously deserted by all of the English colonists.

Despite his determination to solve the mystery, White was prevented from doing so. The captain of the ship in which White had returned to Roanoke at first agreed to take the governor on a search along the coast, but again a hurricane intervened. Fearing that his ship as well as the other supply vessels might be destroyed, the captain ordered the tiny fleet to sail back to England. There White lived only a few years, dying in despair over his lost family and the other lost colonists.

What happened to the lost colony of Roanoke has not been determined to this day. Although he had spent much of his fortune in a futile attempt to found an English colony in America, Raleigh continued to send out expeditions in search of the lost colony. They met with no success.

Historians have offered many solutions to the mystery, none of them wholly satisfactory. Some historians have said the settlers were killed by Indians. Others have suggested that the Spaniards, who had been raided by Drake at St. Augustine, came up from Florida and destroyed the colony. It has even been speculated that the colonists tried to return to England in one of the ships that White had left with them and were lost at sea in a storm.

Perhaps the most accurate theory is based on the word CROATOAN that was found carved on the trunk of a tree. Some time after the disaster it was learned that Manteo, the friendly Indian, had originally come from an island named Croatoan. Possibly he took the colonists there to obtain aid from his people. The colonists who survived may have intermarried among the Indians. Lending weight to this theory is the fact that as late as the 18th century there was a tribe in the area known as the Hatteras Indians, many of whom had gray eyes—which were found among no other tribes—and said that their ancestors had been white people. Today many of the so-called Croatans of eastern North Carolina have English names and claim to be descendants of the members of the lost colony of Roanoke.

Although Raleigh's attempts to establish a permanent English colony in the New World met with failure, his efforts gave the impetus to successful settlement. The Father of English America was Sir Walter Raleigh; and the birthplace of English America was Roanoke Island.

Raleigh always said, "I shall yet live to see Virginia an English nation." This he did, but the first permanent English settlement was founded not at Roanoke but at Jamestown.

Jamestown, Virginia—named for King James I, who succeeded Elizabeth on the English throne—was founded on May 14, 1607. The Jamestown colonists suffered from the same hardships as those on Roanoke Island—famine, sickness, disputes with the Indians. They were held together by the great strength and determination of Captain John Smith, one of the governors of the colony.

Captain Smith was not only successful in dealing with the Indians for corn and other needed supplies, but he also virtually forced the colonists to raise their own crops. He did this by issuing and enforcing his own order, "He who will not work shall not eat."

According to one romantic legend, Smith was captured by hostile Indians who were about to club him to death when Pocahontas, the daughter of a chief named Powhatan, threw her arms around Smith's neck to protect him. Powhatan was so impressed with the courage of his daughter's act that he spared Smith's life. The truth of this story is somewhat doubtful, but there is no doubting Smith's importance to the colony of Jamestown. Without his leadership the colony would never have survived.

In a shrewd diplomatic gesture, Smith had King James I crown Powhatan king of the Virginia territory in 1609, and presented the chief with a number of valuable gifts. This gesture plus the marriage of Powhatan's daughter, Pocahontas, to an Englishman named John Rolfe helped preserve peace between the colonists and Indians for several years.

Powhatan died, however, in 1618 and was succeeded by his brother, Opechancanough, who hated the English and was determined to drive them into the sea. This determination led to two bloody assaults by Opechancanough's tribes against the Virginia settlers, one in

1622 and the other in 1644. In the first assault seventy-two of the colony's eighty small settlements were destroyed along with some 350 settlers. In the second, some 500 men, women and children were killed.

The white man did his best to repay the Indian in kind. Between the two Indian uprisings, the settlers invited Opechancanough and his chiefs to a treaty council to talk peace. Once the Indians were assembled, the white men fell upon them and attempted to slaughter them to the last man. Opechancanough was one of the handful of Indians who escaped with their lives. He was eventually captured by Governor William Berkeley's militia and taken to Jamestown where he was put on display before the curious and revengeful colonists.

While being held prisoner, Opechancanough was shot and mortally wounded by a guard. Before his death the old chief was reported to have demanded to see Governor Berkeley. When the governor arrived, Opechancanough rose from his death bed, pointed an accusing finger at Berkeley and said, "If I had taken William Berkeley prisoner, I never would have put him on display in front of *my* people." The proud old chief then lay down and died.

With the success of the founding of Virginia (1607), English colonies began to be established elsewhere along the eastern seaboard of what is today the United States. These included Massachusetts (1620), New Hampshire (1623), Maryland (1634), Connecticut (1635), Rhode Island (1636), North Carolina (1653),

New Jersey (1664), South Carolina (1670), Pennsylvania (1682) and Georgia (1733). New Netherland (1624) was established by the Dutch but was later taken over by the English and named New York after the Duke of York. Although Delaware (1638) was not founded by the English, it was named after Lord De la Warr, an early governor of Virginia. First the Swedes and then the Dutch ruled the region, which was taken over by the English when they captured New Netherland in 1664.

None of these colonies in America was settled without severe cost and hardship. Countless settlers died of hunger, disease and in conflicts with the Indians. America was, of course, the Indians' homeland and they fought fiercely to protect it from the land-hungry white settlers. Nevertheless, in time a string of thirteen sturdy English colonies stretched from Spanish-held Florida in the south to French-held Canada in the north.

As the English colonies grew, they also came into sharp conflict with their Spanish and French neighbors, especially the latter. A basic cause of this conflict was the struggle over which country should control the North American continent. In Europe, England, France, Spain and their allies were almost constantly at war during this period, and this conflict spilled over into America. The result was a series of colonial wars—King William's War (1689–1697), Queen Anne's War (1702–1713), King George's War (1744–1748), and finally, the French and Indian War (1754–1763).

THE COLONIAL WARS AND THEIR EUROPEAN COUNTERPARTS
1689–1763

In America	In Europe	European Warring Powers	Treaty
King William's War (1689–1697)	War of the Grand Alliance (1688–1697)	France vs. England, Holland, Spain, Austria, Sweden	Ryswick
Queen Anne's War (1702–1713)	War of the Spanish Succession (1701–1713)	France, Spain, Bavaria vs. Great Britain,* Holland, Austria, Portugal, Prussia, etc.	Utrecht
King George's War (1744–1748)	War of the Austrian Succession (1740–1748)	Prussia, France, Spain, Bavaria vs. Austria, Great Britain,* Holland	Aix - la- Chapelle
French and Indian War (1754–1763)	Seven Year's War (1756–1763)	Prussia, Great Britain vs. Austria, France, Russia, Sweden	Paris

*England, Wales and Scotland were officially joined in 1707 to form Great Britain.

Two

*The
Spanish and
French
in
North America*

Any neutral observer watching the early struggle among the major European nations to control North America would probably have voted for England as the nation least likely to succeed. Spain would undoubtedly have been voted the most likely to succeed.

The early Norsemen were the first Europeans to discover America around the year 1000, settling at what is now Newfoundland. It is possible that long before that —as much as 3,500 years ago—the ancestors of certain American Indian tribes came to the Western Hemisphere from lands bordering the southern Mediterranean Sea. But it was Spain that took the lead in exploring the New World following its rediscovery by Christopher Columbus in 1492.

Columbus was an Italian sea captain whose voyages were sponsored by Spain. Interestingly, England's first claims to North America were also based on the voyages of an Italian sea captain—Giovanni Caboto, who has since been known as John Cabot. Cabot, sailing from Bristol, England, discovered Newfoundland on the North American continent in midsummer, 1497.

The Spanish were never as interested as the English later proved to be in establishing permanent colonies along the east coast of North America. They were more interested in seeking treasure—gold, silver and spices. They were also keenly interested in converting the Indians to Catholicism.*

During the 16th century, Spanish explorers in search of treasure roamed across the whole southern part of the area, from the Carolinas to California, that is now known as the United States. These Spanish adventurers were called *conquistadores,* which meant conquerors.

Florida was discovered by Ponce de León in 1513 and named by him; the Spanish word *florida* means "flowery," or "full of flowers." He was later wounded by Indians and taken to Cuba where he died. In 1565, some forty-two years before the English founded Jamestown,

*The first Americans were called *Indians* by Columbus because he thought he had discovered India when he first sighted what are today the Bahama Islands in the West Indies. Other explorers called the Indians "red men" or "redskins" because of the color of their skin. The Indians had no general name for themselves other than a word that meant, "The People," or, "The Men." This term was used freely among the Indians to indicate all of their members.

the Spanish founded St. Augustine, the oldest permanent European settlement on the United States mainland. Somewhat earlier, Hernando de Soto landed at what is today Tampa Bay and then explored the area of the present Gulf States. De Soto, the first white man to sight and cross the Mississippi River, died of a fever and was buried in the Mississippi.

None of these and numerous other Spanish explorers discovered any treasure, however, so the Spanish shifted their efforts elsewhere—mainly to the south and southwest.

Meanwhile, the other major European nations began to be active in their exploration and settlement of North America. The English and French in particular became serious rivals in establishing colonies in the New World. (The Portuguese, Dutch and Swedes also engaged in important early exploration and settlement in North America, but their American colonial empires were relatively short-lived as compared with those of the French and English.)

As with the Spanish, religion played a key role in England's and France's early exploration and colonization. The English Pilgrims came to America to avoid religious persecution, and the French missionaries came to convert the Indians to Catholicism. (The English also made efforts to convert the "pagan" red men, but it was not one of their primary purposes for coming to the New World as it was with the French missionaries.) National rivalry also played a role, but the main reason for colonization was strictly economic. Colonies were sources of wealth for the mother countries.

Colonies produced raw materials that were shipped to the mother country where they were manufactured into goods that were in turn sold back to the colonies. Colonies were owned by the countries that founded them, and they were allowed to do little or no trading with rival nations. This was called *mercantilism.* Mercantilism, or the Mercantile System, was based on the theory that a nation would prosper if it exported more goods than it imported, thus bringing in more money from goods sold than was spent for goods bought. This theory is still held to be true today by the major nations of the world.

While this attitude of self-interest on the part of the major nations of Europe during the 16th and 17th centuries helped make possible the early permanent settlement of the New World, it also led in time to such violent reactions as the American Revolution. It also established a pattern of so-called Colonialism that has continued to be a major cause of controversy throughout the world up to the present day.

Among the most important raw materials found in early North America were furs, especially beaver furs. Fish, and particularly codfish, were also a valuable source of revenue from the New World's offshore waters. It was the French who took the lead in establishing the early fur trade as the richest source of overseas income for the mother country.

As early as 1524, Francis I of France sent another Italian sea captain, Giovanni da Verrazano, on an expedition to the New World. Verrazano explored the east coast of North America from what is today the Carolinas to modern Newfoundland, thus giving France a strong claim to North America.

In 1534, King Francis sent Jacques Cartier on the first of several expeditions to North America, during the course of which he explored the Gulf of St. Lawrence and sailed up the St. Lawrence to the present site of Montreal. Cartier named the height behind the site Mont Réal.

These early explorations were followed by numerous unsuccessful attempts to establish French colonies to exploit the New World fur trade. It was not, however, until 1608, one year after the English founded Jamestown, that Samuel de Champlain sailed into the lower St. Lawrence and founded Quebec. This was the first permanent French colony established in North America. From Quebec the French gradually fanned out into the North American heartland, setting up forts and fur trading posts as they went.

One of the most famous of these French explorers of the North American interior was René Robert Cavelier, *sieur* (sir) de La Salle, the first white man to journey down the Mississippi River to the Gulf of Mexico in 1682. Earlier, in 1673, Louis Joliet and Father Jacques Marquette had also explored the upper Mississippi, but it was La Salle who first voyaged to the great river's mouth. Ironically, it was La Salle's inability to find again the mouth of the Mississippi on a later voyage that led to his death.

Returning from a trip to France in 1684, La Salle sailed into the Gulf of Mexico, searched in vain for the entry to the lower Mississippi, and when he could not find it, set off on an overland journey toward the north to join one of his aides, Henri de Tonti, who was stationed in the Illinois country. Tonti, La Salle's most faithful lieutenant during his early New World explorations, was called "the man with the iron hand" by the Indians. This was because one of Tonti's hands had been blown off in battle and in its place he wore a metal claw.

La Salle's desperate overland journey to rejoin Tonti had a tragic ending. On March 19, 1687, La Salle was slain by several of his mutinous men. Tonti lived on to see La Salle recognized as the Father of the Louisiana Territory.

The French founded New Orleans in 1718. It soon became a major base from which supplies could be shipped to trading posts and settlements as far north as Quebec and Montreal in New France, as Canada was then called. With this string of forts and trading posts the French not only controlled the North American fur trade, but they also threatened to control the whole of what is today the St. Lawrence, Ohio and Mississippi Valley area, which was the key to the control of the North American continent.

The early thirteen English colonies, on the other hand, were actually nothing more than a beachhead along the eastern seaboard—a beachhead that was threatened by the French whose settlements ranged from Canada in the north to New Orleans in the south. It seemed apparent that at any time they wanted to do so, the French could drive the English out of their beachhead colonies and into the sea.

As this menacing situation grew, conflict between England and France in the New World became inevitable. A key question from the very beginning of this almost century-long series of conflicts was which nation would have the North American Indians on its side.

At this time, there were only slightly more than one million native Americans, or Indians, living in the vast, sprawling wilderness of North America. These relatively few people, however, were to wield an influence that was far greater than mere numbers in shaping the course of American history during the Colonial Wars.

When the French and British had first come to North America, they were greeted in friendly fashion by the Indians. The Indians not only traded with the white men, but they also taught the newcomers what crops to plant, how to build the best kinds of shelter, how and where to fish and hunt, and how to find their way through the trackless wilderness. The red men welcomed these white-skinned strangers from across the sea much as they might welcome any other friendly newcomers to their tribal territories.

In return the Indians eventually were debauched with rum by the white man and driven from their lands and homes.

For a time after the coming of the white man, however, the Indians prospered due to the introduction of new tools and weapons. These were fashioned from iron and steel, and their use enabled the Indians to spend more time in leisure and in religious ceremonies. With the white man's gun, for example, it was much easier for the Indians to obtain food than with bows and arrows or snares. It also, unfortunately, made it much easier for the Indians to conduct war and was influential in aiding the Iroquois to maintain a virtual empire in New York, Pennsylvania and the Ohio Valley.

The government of the Iroquois empire, or Confederacy as it was called, might well have served as a model for the freedom-seeking New Englanders, especially since many of its laws were remarkably democratic. Women of the Confederacy, for example, were allowed to vote and to own property. The various tribes of the Confederacy formed a loose federation not unlike the later federation of the thirteen Colonies in which elected representatives met in assembly to vote on solutions to various problems.

Powerful as it was before the coming of the white man, the Iroquois Confederacy sought to further extend its control over its Indian neighbors through use of guns and gunpowder, once these were available. Both the French and English exploited this demand for weapons by seducing the Indians with rum, religion and any other available means.

The Indians also fell prey to new diseases to which they were not immune. Smallpox was especially devastating to the native Americans, a fact which was not lost sight of by the conquering white man. No less an outstanding soldier than England's Lord Jeffrey Amherst, at one stage of the Colonial Wars, was apparently responsible for distributing blankets infected with smallpox to the Delaware Indians at Fort Pitt, an action that resulted in a smallpox epidemic among the Indians.

In competing with each other for control of trade in North America—and thus for control of the North American continent itself—both the English and French knew they would have to have a majority of the Indians on their side if they were going to win. In the beginning, however, it was strictly a series of fights between the white man and the red man, and in these conflicts the odds were all against the latter.

Three

*White Man
Against
Red Man*

When Champlain founded Quebec* in 1608, he brought
with him the first steel armor and the first firearms the
Indians in this area had ever seen. These Indians were
the Algonquins, whose ancient enemies were the fierce
and warlike Iroquois, or Five Confederate Nations, many
of whom lived in what is now the state of New York. No
one knew why the Algonquins and the Iroquois were
always at war with one another. The reasons for their
continuing conflict were lost in the mists of history.

Champlain's firearms were arquebuses, a kind of

---

*From a similar Indian word meaning a strait, or where the waters narrow.

short, heavy musket. Although the arquebus was usually fired from a gun rest placed on the ground, this primitive musket was well suited for firing in the forest and was deadly at short range. When the Algonquins saw these "thunderhorns" fired for the first time and noted the damage they could do, they urged Champlain and his men to join them in an attack against the Iroquois.

At first, Champlain, the Father of New France, was reluctant to do so. Up to this time the French had maintained more or less friendly relations with the Indians. This was mainly due to the fact that, unlike the English, the French did not threaten the Indians' lands. Few of the early French came to North America to stay. They came "for gold, for glory, and for the love of God," as they described their efforts. Translated, this "musket-and-cross" philosophy meant that the French came to North America for beaver furs and to convert the Indians to Catholicism.

Since they were not primarily interested in establishing permanent colonies in the New World, many of the French traders simply scattered out and lived among the Indians in their villages, adopting their way of life, taking Indian brides, and in general accepting the red men and being accepted by them as complete equals. In fact, many sons of French fathers and Indian mothers became every bit as expert as woodsmen and warriors as were their full-blooded Indian teachers. These half-breed bushrangers whose prowess rivaled that of the full-blooded Indian braves were called *coureurs de bois,* or runners of the forest. When war eventually broke out between the French and the English for the control of the North American continent, the English feared and respected the runners of the forest more than they did any other enemy.

The Algonquins continued to urge Champlain to join them in battle against their bitter enemies. Finally, in the spring of 1609, he agreed to do so. His purpose was to prove to the Indian tribes of Canada that he was their close ally and leader. If he could unite the Canadian Indians and gain their loyalty, French control of the New World would be assured.

Champlain left Quebec late in June with a small party of Frenchmen and several hundred Indians. They traveled in Indian birchbark canoes. The journey was both a long and a difficult one. All day long, from dawn to dark, the men paddled their canoes through the lush, green tunnel formed by the trees that arched over the St. Lawrence river. It was hot, tiring work and at night, immediately after eating, the men went quickly to sleep in their riverside camp.

As they neared the enemy no fires were permitted, so the evening meal and breakfast the next day had to be cold, dried meat or fish and cornmeal. Each night the camp also had to be camouflaged. This was done by stripping elm bark from the trees and spreading it over the tops of the tents.

In the third week of the journey, the party was forced to make a long portage around some river rapids. Unwilling to carry their canoes on this portage, a number of the Indians decided to return to Quebec. But Champlain stubbornly pressed on. Finally, they entered what was later called Lake Champlain, and here, on the late afternoon of July 29, they encountered the enemy in a flotilla of canoes.

As soon as they saw Champlain's war party, the Iroquois put in to shore, not wanting to do battle on the lake. There they hastily began to erect a log barricade.

Champlain and his party remained in their canoes. As dusk fell, the Algonquins lashed their canoes together to form a kind of platform on the waters of the lake. All night long Champlain's Indians danced a war dance on this makeshift platform.

At dawn the next morning Champlain and two of his aides put on their metal armor. Over their doublets and long stockings went breastplates, backpieces, and thin steel thigh protectors called cuisses. Finally they donned plumed, steel helmets.

As the Algonquins began to paddle toward shore, Champlain and his armored aides, each gripping his arquebus, and covered with Indian robes lay on the bottom of their canoes. In a few moments the canoes reached the shore, their bottoms scraping on the gravel of the beach, and Champlain and his men sprang out. They had landed several hundred yards from the enemy, but almost immediately the Iroquois began to file from behind their barricade and advance upon Champlain and the Algonquins.

The Iroquois were some two hundred strong—against less than half that many in Champlain's party—two hundred of the most feared warriors in North America. They were led by three chiefs wearing elaborate, feathered headdresses. The chiefs also wore armor and carried shields. Their armor and shields were made of interwoven twigs and covered with cloth, and were meant to serve as protection against arrows.

At first, a protective screen of Algonquins strode forward in front of Champlain and his two French aides. As the Iroquois approached, however, the Algonquins stood aside and let Champlain move forward to face the enemy unprotected.

"I looked at them," Champlain wrote afterward in describing the action, "and they looked at me. When I saw that they were getting ready to shoot their arrows at us, I leveled my arquebus, which I had loaded with four balls, and aimed straight at the three chiefs. The shot brought down two of them. Our Indians then set up such a yelling that one could not have heard a thunderclap, and all the while the arrows flew thick on both sides. The Iroquois were greatly frightened to see two of their chiefs killed so quickly, despite their arrow-proof armor."

As Champlain was reloading, his two companions fired their arquebuses and brought down the third chief. This caused the Iroquois to flee into the nearby forest. The Algonquins followed in hot pursuit. Many of the Iroquois were killed and most of the others captured.

That night, as was the Indian custom, the Algonquins tortured their prisoners, scalping some of them alive, and then eating their hearts and drinking their blood. By so doing, they believed they would gain the strength and courage of their enemies.

The next day, as he left the scene of his triumph, Champlain congratulated himself for having attained such a total victory. It was, however, a victory that he would in many ways live to regret, for it united the Five Nations of the Iroquois as nothing else could have done. In the months and years that followed the Iroquois—often goaded into action by the English—were to reap a bloody revenge against Champlain and the other leaders of New France in the New World.

The French, for their part, encouraged their Indian allies to take the warpath against the English, pointing out again and again how the red men's lands were being taken over by the British colonists. Much of what the French told the Indians was true, although the English did not see it in this light.

Like the French, the early English in North America were interested in trade, but they mainly wanted to settle on and own this new land. They were willing to be fair about such ownership—fair, that is, in the western European sense of the word. This meant buying and paying for whatever land they wanted and the Indians were willing to sell. The only problem was that the Indians did not understand the European idea of land ownership.

Basically, the Indians had no sense of property. Often they would sell a piece of land to the English but continue to hunt and fish in the area just as they always had done in the past. When the English who had bought the land objected to the Indians' continued presence on it, the Indians quite literally did not know what it was that the British were objecting to. All through the colonial period, there was constant friction between the land-hungry English colonists and the Indians.

An early quarrel broke out in 1637 between the Connecticut colonists and a group of Pequot Indians. When a white trader—who had mistreated the Indians—was murdered, the colonists attacked a Pequot village near Mystic and killed some 600 Indians. Also during the early 17th century, there was fighting between Virginia colonists and the Indians. There a Powhatan chief led his people against the English settlers along the James River. They massacred the settlers of Jamestown in 1622, and in 1644 they killed more than 300 white settlers.

Perhaps the most tragic conflict between the British colonists and the Indians, however, was King Philip's War, which began in 1675 and lasted for more than a year.

When the Pilgrims first settled in the New World, one of their best friends among the Indians was Massasoit, chief of the Wampanoags. Massasoit thought so much of the Pilgrims that he asked them to give his two sons English names. Thus, one son was named Alexander and the other Philip.

When Massasoit died in 1661, Alexander became chief of the Wampanoags. Unlike his father, Alexander did not wholly trust the British. Because Alexander showed no signs of friendship toward them, the colonists feared he might be plotting with the French to attack them.

Colonial soldiers brought him to Plymouth to swear allegiance to the English, which he refused to do. While being held prisoner, Alexander became ill and died.

Philip, Alexander's brother, now became chief of the Wampanoags, and he swore to avenge Alexander's death. Although he was only in his early twenties, Philip was a great leader. For a dozen years, he worked to unite the Indian tribes of New England into a federation to defeat the white man once and for all. The various Indian tribes, however, were not used to uniting under a single leader. Each tribe preferred to remain independent under its own chief. Nevertheless, King Philip, as he soon was called by the colonists, was more successful in his effort to unite the Indians than any chief before him had been. (Afterwards the Ottawa chief, Pontiac, an ally of the French, was to be successful in uniting many tribes in the middle west against the British. And Tecumseh, probably the most successful of all the Indian leaders in uniting his people, played a key role in the War of 1812. Tecumseh's story is told in another book in this series— *The War of 1812: America's Second War for Independence.*)

One of King Philip's trusted aides was another Indian who had been named by the English. This was John Sassamon. Sassamon, despite his sworn allegiance to Philip, was an informer. He revealed to the colonists all of Philip's war plans. While Sassamon was on one of his informer's missions in Plymouth in 1675, he was murdered. The colonists blamed Philip for this murder, and they hanged three Wampanoags for the crime. Although this single act precipitated the bloody war that followed, there were other harsh and unreasonable measures taken earlier by the colonists that had angered the Indians. For example, the colonists attempted to force the red men to observe Sunday as a holy day, and any Indian using profanity was subject to capital punishment.

King Philip's War involved not only the Wampanoags but also the Nipmucks and the Narragansetts—about 12,000 Indians—against some 40,000 armed white settlers in the whole of New England. For many months the war raged up and down the Connecticut Valley—through Massachusetts, Plymouth and Rhode Island. The Indians killed men, women and children in their raids on the white settlements. The colonists struck back with equally barbarous attacks against the Indians. Scalps were taken on both sides. Captive Indians were either slaughtered or sold into slavery.

Gradually, however, the white man's superiority in numbers, weapons and supplies began to prove too much for the Indians. The red men had to live off the land and fight a kind of guerrilla warfare. With no time to hunt game or to plant crops, the Indian braves and their families slowly began to starve. Nevertheless, they fought on.

Finally in August of 1676, King Philip and the remnants of his war parties retreated to a swamp in Rhode Island. There they were hunted down like animals and killed.

With the death of King Philip, the tragic war that bore his name ended in southern New England. It continued fitfully in northern New England for a few more months.

The New Englanders of this era never forgave King Philip and his native followers for their roles in this war. As late as 1700, King Philip's severed head was still on display, mounted on a pole at Plymouth, and the remnants of his people, who were regarded as the agents of Satan, were sold into slavery in the West Indies.

It was now clear that when the French and the British began to fight each other neither would have the Indians wholly on their side.

The French and British began to fight each other in 1689, in King William's War.

Four

*King William's
War*

A French professional soldier and an American colonial sailor played the lead roles in the opening acts of King William's War. The French soldier was Count Louis de Frontenac. The colonial sailor, fighting for the British against the French, was Sir William Phips.

When Frontenac was first made governor of Canada in 1672, he bore the numerous scars of battle from a lifetime of fighting for his king and country. Born near Paris in 1620, he saw his first service as a soldier in the Netherlands at the age of fifteen. Later he fought in Italy and Germany. By the time he had reached his late teens, he was highly regarded as a combat leader; in his mid-twenties he became a general in the French army. But Frontenac's great problem was in making and keeping friends. He had, in fact, a positive genius for making enemies.

In his first term as governor of Canada, Frontenac was highly successful in several ways. After their defeat by Champlain, the Iroquois quickly recovered and made a series of murderous raids against the French in Canada. Frontenac reorganized the Canadian military forces and, over a period of years, the French with their Indian allies so thoroughly defeated the Iroquois that they were never again a serious threat. In addition, Frontenac built up the fur trade to its most successful level; he also established some forms of self-government in Quebec.

Along the way, however, Frontenac antagonized so many high officials, including a number of Jesuit priests, that he was finally recalled to France.

The War of the Grand Alliance broke out in Europe in 1688. Although there were other nations involved, this was essentially a war between England and France, with England trying to keep France from gaining control of the whole of western Europe. When this European conflict threatened to spill over into America, Frontenac was hastily returned to Canada to serve his second term as governor. He was in office only a few months when King William's War began, and Frontenac made immediate plans to attack the New England colonies. (It was called King William's War in America because William III was on the English throne).

The leader of the English colonial forces was Sir William "Lucky Billy" Phips, one of the most colorful figures in early American history. Phips had been born in 1651 at Pemaquid, Maine. He was the twenty-first child of twenty-six children born to the same mother. Some people said that because three times seven, or twenty-one, was considered to be lucky, Phips was lucky from the day he was born.

As a boy Billy Phips worked as a shepherd and later as a ship's carpenter. While working aboard ships in Boston harbor, he heard many tales about Spanish galleons filled with gold that had been sunk off the Bahama Islands. Finally, in 1687, he organized an expedition to find one of these ships and recover its cargo of sunken treasure. Although his first trip was unsuccessful, on his second trip Phips found a wrecked galleon in shallow water off the Bahamas and recovered some £300,000 (more than a million dollars) in gold, silver and jewels. He took his prize to England, where he became the first American to be knighted. Later, rich and famous, he returned to Boston.

When King William's War broke out, Phips was not yet forty years old. Frontenac, on the other hand, was seventy—but he acted like a man half that age as he readied his French-Canadian forces to attack the English colonists in New York, New Hampshire and Maine.

In the winter of 1690, about two hundred Canadians (many of them the feared *coureurs de bois*) and their Indian allies left Montreal and crossed frozen Lake Champlain. The attack was aimed at the frontier outpost of Schenectady, about fifteen miles from Albany, New York. Here some 200 colonists and their black slaves lived in a stockaded village.

Frontenac's forces wore snowshoes and pulled their supplies on sleds. They arrived at Schenectady on the night of February 8. Much to the Canadians' surprise, the gates to the village were wide open. Curiously, the only guards were two solitary snowmen.

Silently the Canadian forces filed into the town. As soon as they had surrounded all of the log cabins, they went to work systematically killing the sleeping occupants—men, women and children. Within an hour sixty settlers and a dozen blacks were killed and the rest of the inhabitants were taken prisoner. Only two of the invaders were killed.

After setting fire to the village, the Canadians fled, taking most of the prisoners, including five blacks, with them. The next day, colonists from Albany and a party of Mohawk braves formed a pursuit party, but the Canadians made their way safely back to Montreal.

Before any colonial resistance could be organized, Frontenac's forces struck again. This time their target was Salmon Falls near Portsmouth, New Hampshire. The attacking party of some fifty Canadians and Indians left Trois Rivières in southeast Canada in early March, and on March 18 smashed into the stockaded New Hampshire village, where they killed more than thirty townspeople and captured more than fifty others.

Frontenac's third attack was launched against Fort Loyal on Casco Bay at what is now Portland, Maine. This attacking party included several hundred Abnaki Indians. It was reinforced by the party of French and Indians who were returning to Canada from Salmon Falls.

At Fort Loyal, Frontenac's forces did not achieve complete surprise, mainly because they were too eager to attack and so killed a lone colonist a mile outside the fort. The scalping shouts that went up as the Indians fell upon their solitary victim alerted the garrison. Foolishly, some thirty of the fort's defenders left the safety of the stockade and attacked the Indians. They were killed and scalped to the last man.

The commander of Fort Loyal, Captain Sylvanus Davis, saw that resistance was useless and offered to surrender if he and his people were given safe conduct to a nearby town. The French readily—too readily—agreed. No sooner were the men, women and children outside the fortress walls than the Indians set upon them with tomahawks and scalping knives. Only a handful of captives, including Captain Davis, were taken as prisoners to Quebec.

After Frontenac's attacks on Schenectady and Salmon Falls, the colony of Massachusetts decided to move independently against the French. One of the curious aspects of this early colonial period was the fact that the colonies made little effort to cooperate with one another. When one colony was threatened or actually attacked, the other colonies were frequently indifferent to their neighbor's fate. Real cooperation would only come later when unity was forged in the fires of the American Revolution.

Now, however, the Massachusetts colonists out of a

sheer sense of self-preservation decided to mount a major amphibious assault against the French in Acadia (Nova Scotia). Massachusetts shipping had frequently been attacked by French warships sailing out of Acadia's Port Royal. Officials of the Bay Colony decided the time was long overdue to destroy this threat to their economic survival once and for all. Given command of this expedition was Sir William Phips.

Phips' command consisted of about 300 sailors and some 500 militia aboard seven ships. This amphibious force reached Port Royal in May, 1690, and it was immediately apparent that Phips' legendary luck was still with him. Inside a tumbledown fort there were less than a hundred defenders. They surrendered almost immediately. Phips destroyed the fort as well as several other outposts along the coast. He also made the Canadians take an oath of allegiance to the British Crown and the colonial officials of Massachusetts. He then returned to Boston to announce his capture of the whole of Acadia.

Back in Boston, Phips received a hero's welcome and was immediately put in command of a seaborne expedition to capture Quebec. Meanwhile, the New York colonists were mounting a simultaneous land attack against Montreal.

Several of the colonies tentatively agreed to furnish troops for this overland expedition. New York agreed to furnish 400 men, Massachusetts 160, Connecticut 135, Maryland 100 and Plymouth 60. The Iroquois offered to contribute 800 warriors to the effort.

Even this relatively modest force never materialized. Massachusetts, Plymouth and Maryland failed to contribute any troops. New York and Connecticut managed to meet only a fraction of their quotas, and an epidemic of smallpox prevented all but a few Indians from joining the expedition.

Both the English colonists and the French Canadians expected help from their mother countries in this venture, but this aid also failed to materialize. Generally speaking, both England and France were inclined to let their countrymen fend for themselves in the New World when war broke out. The mother countries tended to "let Americans fight Americans."

In the end, the overland expedition against Montreal proved to be a complete failure.

The seaborne expedition led by Sir William Phips against Quebec began much more auspiciously. Massachusetts contributed more than 2,000 men and some thirty-four ships to the effort.

The fleet sailed in mid-August and was joined by three more ships from New York. Due to adverse winds and the lack of a pilot who knew the St. Lawrence River, it took the small armada about two months to reach Quebec. Here Count Frontenac and a force of several thousand Canadians and their Indian allies awaited the invasion.

Frontenac had left Quebec and hastened to Montreal, when that city had seemed to be threatened by the proposed New York land expedition. When this part of the dual attack on Canada failed, however, Frontenac had quickly returned to Quebec and strengthened his defenses there. Now he was more than ready for Phips' attempt at a seaborne invasion. And now, for the first time, Lucky Billy Phips' luck ran out.

Arriving at Quebec, Phips sent a note ashore to Frontenac, demanding his immediate surrender.

Frontenac's reply quickly arrived aboard Phips' flagship: "I am not a man to be summoned in such fashion. You do your best, and I will do mine."

Phips' immediate response was to land some 1,300 troops under the command of Major John Walley at a point downriver from Quebec. These troops were to move inland, cross the St. Charles River and attack the city from the rear. Meanwhile, the fleet would bombard the fortress from the front.

A series of near disasters soon followed. By now the weather had turned to freezing cold. Smallpox struck down many of the expedition's men, and Phips failed to get enough food and ammunition ashore for Major Walley's forces. These troops did manage, however, to remain ashore in the frozen mud for several days, although they were able to make only a modest advance against the rear of Quebec.

Phips attempted to bombard the fortress into submission, but since it sat high atop a rocky cliff, Phips' gunners had little luck in firing up at it. The French, on the other hand, could rake the decks of the attacking fleet with devastating effect whenever the ships came within range of the fortress guns.

In the end, Phips had to call off the attack, rescue

Walley's men from the shore and sail sadly back to Boston where he arrived in November.

Although Phips did not return to a hero's welcome after this expedition, the devout people of the Bay Colony did not blame him. They blamed the failure on God, the weather and the fortunes of war.

As a result of the failure of Phips' expedition, Massachusetts found itself virtually bankrupt. The colonists had hoped to pay for the effort with the spoils taken when Quebec was captured. Now, however, they found themselves £50,000 in debt. To meet this emergency, paper money was issued and taxes were increased to make good the values printed on the face of the money. This was the first time paper money was issued in America. It was a device that would be used to finance all of America's future wars.

Sir William Phips' capture of Port Royal in Acadia and his failure to capture Frontenac's citadel at Quebec were the only major military actions of King William's War. And, in the end, the former effort proved to be as much of a failure as the latter. For when Phips left Port Royal in Acadia, he left no garrison behind him. Consequently, the oath of allegiance he made the Canadians take to the British Crown and Massachusetts officials was completely ignored.

"When Phips left," the Acadians said, "he carried his oath with him."

And in 1697 when the English and French ended the War of the Grand Alliance in Europe, the peace treaty that was signed at Ryswick, Holland, had as one of its provisions the return of Acadia to France. Actually, the war in Europe and the war in North America had settled very little.

The war did, however, drag on for a number of years after the failure of the Quebec expedition, but the closing military actions were much like the actions that opened the conflict—small but bloody raids and massacres along the border between New England and French Canada.

The exposed area of French Canada extended along the St. Lawrence River for a distance of less than one hundred miles. The exposed frontier of New England, on the other hand, was several hundred miles long and was made up of scattered farms and small villages.

During the last years of the war, a series of forts were built by the colonists to protect the New England frontier. In charge of this defense program was none other than Sir William Phips, who had not only been forgiven for his Quebec fiasco by King William, but had now also been named the governor of Massachusetts.

One of the first of these defensive outposts built by Phips was near his birthplace at Pemaquid, Maine. It was named Fort William Henry after the English king. Constructed of stone rather than logs and strategically situated so that it served as a shield to protect Boston from Canadian raids from the north, Fort William was a constant challenge to Frontenac. He knew that if Fort William could be captured the whole of New England would be vulnerable to the French and their Indian allies.

In July, 1696, the French attacked Fort William and the garrison commander, Captain Pascoe Chubb, surrendered without firing any of his fifteen cannon. Captain Chubb was later court-martialed, but the damage had apparently been done.

Frontenac immediately made plans to mount a major seaborne attack against Boston. The key to this amphibious assault was a squadron of fifteen French warships in which Frontenac's forces would be transported from Quebec. Now, however, it was Frontenac's turn to have his luck run out. The warships sailed from France but were becalmed for weeks in mid-Atlantic. When one lone ship arrived at Quebec with the news that the French fleet had run low on provisions and had been forced to return to France, Frontenac said that never again would he have such an ideal opportunity to destroy the English in North America. He was right. A year later the seventy-eight-year-old governor was dead.

Meanwhile, however, many small bands of French and Indians, especially the latter, carried out a series of savage raids against the New England settlers. The settlers retaliated as best they could, but it was a dark and bloody time indeed for the English colonists who clung with such a desperately thin grip to the eastern rim of the North American continent.

Not only men but women also learned how to fight for their lives and ask no quarter in this grim struggle. Hannah Dustin, a farm woman living in the village of Haverhill, Massachusetts, was a typical example of such a woman.

One spring morning about a year after the fall of Fort William Henry, a band of Abnaki Indians attacked several farmhouses at Haverhill. In one of the houses lay Hannah Dustin who had given birth to her eighth child just a few days earlier. Her neighbor, Mary Neff, was also in the house acting as a nurse.

Hannah's husband, Thomas Dustin, was working in one of the nearby fields and had the other seven Dustin children with him. At the first sound of the Indian attack, Thomas ordered his children to run to a fortified house about a mile away. Then, seizing his gun, he mounted his horse and rode toward the village. By the time he arrived, however, the farmhouses were all ablaze and the Indian war party was making its escape. Assuming that his wife and baby had been killed, Thomas now thought only of saving his remaining children and rode off to join them.

Hannah Dustin had not been slain, however. She and Mary Neff were taken prisoner. But the baby was killed before its mother's eyes by an Indian who dashed the newborn infant against a tree.

Hannah Dustin, Mary Neff and an English boy named Samuel Lenorson were turned over to a family of Indians that was headed toward an Abnaki village some 250 miles from Haverhill. The family consisted of three braves, two squaws and seven children. Along the way, the captives were told that when they reached their destination they would be beaten, made to run the gauntlet naked and otherwise tortured.

Hannah made up her mind that they must escape as

soon as possible or none of the three would see their homes again. Mary and Samuel agreed to join Hannah in her attempt to escape. The farther they progressed on their journey the less closely the Indians guarded their prisoners. The captives were many miles from any white settlements, and even if they escaped, there was little chance of finding their way home.

One night when they had traveled about halfway to their destination Hannah, Mary and the boy remained awake until all of the Indians had fallen asleep. Hannah had previously stolen and hidden a tomahawk and the other two prisoners now stealthily took hatchets from the sleeping warriors. Then all three struck at once, smashing the bare heads of several of the sleeping Indians. They struck again, and yet again, before the rest of their captors were fully aroused. They succeeded in killing ten of the twelve Indians, an old squaw and a small boy managing to make their terrified escape into the forest.

Hannah and her companions waited by the dead Indians until daylight. Then Hannah methodically scalped all of the victims. Taking muskets and as much food with them as they could carry, the trio started back toward Haverhill where they arrived several weeks later. Hannah's husband was, of course, unbelievably surprised to see his wife alive and well. He was even more surprised to see the ten trophies she brought him, trophies for which Massachusetts later awarded Mrs. Dustin £50, which was the standard bounty for Indian scalps.

Five

Queen Anne's War

The Treaty of Ryswick ending the War of the Grand Alliance in Europe was signed on September 30, 1697. News of the signing of the treaty did not reach the English colonists until December, and the French Canadians did not hear the good news until February, 1698.

There then followed a shaky truce, both in Europe and in North America, that was to last for just five years. The New England colonists and the French Canadians used this period to prepare for a renewal of the conflict which everyone was certain would sooner or later occur. Once again the war was to start in Europe and spill over into America.

The cause of the new European conflict was a dispute over who should rule Spain, and that country's possessions, following the death of the childless Spanish king, Charles II, in 1700. King Charles had wanted to be succeeded on the throne by his grandnephew, Philip, a member of the French royal family.

Philip's claim to the Spanish throne was challenged by several European nations that supported the Archduke Charles of Austria's claim to the throne. England, fearing that a union between France and Spain would destroy the balance of power in Europe, supported Charles's claim. The War of the Spanish Succession actually began in Europe in 1701, but England did not declare war against France and Spain until May 4, 1702.

In America the conflict, which also began in 1702, was called Queen Anne's War. Queen Anne had succeeded her brother-in-law, King William, on the English throne when the latter died following a fall from his horse.

The renewal of war in America brought an immediate renewal of the murderous border raids by the French who encouraged the Indians to attack the English. Settlers in New England—mainly those in Massachusetts—once again had to face the daily threat of being scalped, captured and tortured to death, or kept as permanent prisoners. Hundreds of the colonists saw their homes and isolated villages burned to the ground, and their crops and livestock destroyed.

The village of Wells, Maine, was the first to suffer the scourge of the Abnaki Indians goaded on by the French.

(Maine was a dependency of Massachusetts during this period.) Casco and other nearby settlements were also destroyed. There soon followed an attack on Deerfield, Massachusetts, in which more than fifty settlers were killed and more than a hundred others were taken as prisoners to Canada. The journey to Canada turned into a death march as the Indians began to kill any of the prisoners who faltered along the way. Some twenty captives, including several black slaves, died in this way.

Among those taken prisoner were a minister, John Williams, his wife and their black slave. Williams's wife and the slave were among those slain on the death march, but Williams survived both the march and a long period of imprisonment as well. In time, he was ransomed and upon his return to New England wrote a book about his adventures, *The Redeemed Captive Returning to Zion*, that was an early colonial best seller for many years after the war. Some sixteen editions of it were published.

It was the Deerfield massacre that succeeded in fully arousing New England. The English colonists now came to the conclusion that the only way they were going to be allowed to live in peace was to drive the French right off the continent. The problem was how to do it, since mounting a major campaign against the French seemed an almost impossible task.

At first, an attack against Quebec was considered but temporarily discarded. Two futile attacks were actually launched against Port Royal in Acadia (Nova Scotia). Major Benjamin Church, a veteran of early Indian fighting during King Philip's War, led the first offensive against Port Royal, but he had only a handful of men and when his demand to surrender was ignored, he returned to Boston. An interesting fact about Major Church was his enormous weight. He was actually so fat that when traveling through the forest, he had to have two aides accompany him to lift him over fallen trees.

When a second attempt against Port Royal led by Colonel John March also met with failure, the English colonists decided they would have to obtain aid from their mother country or admit abject defeat. To obtain this aid, a party of colonists led by Colonel Francis Nicholson and Captain Samuel Vetch sailed for England. With them they took several Mohawk chiefs.

Queen Anne and her court were intrigued by the Indians. Men, ships and supplies were promised Nicholson and Vetch for their all-out campaign against Port Royal.

In July, 1710, half a dozen English warships arrived at Boston. With them was a fighting force of several hundred British marines. New England supplemented this force with some 1,500 men and more than thirty boats in which to transport this amphibious force.

Nicholson's and Vetch's armada reached Port Royal in late September. The soldiers' landing was unopposed, but once ashore they began to suffer from intense cannon and musket fire from the French inside the main fortress. Nicholson and Vetch then laid siege to the fort, and within a few days the French were requesting a chance to surrender honorably. Nicholson accepted the request and the French filed from the fort, flags flying and a band playing, for the very last time. Port Royal was now permanently in English hands. On the morning of the surrender, the English officers entertained the French officers and their ladies at a victory breakfast. Port Royal was renamed Annapolis Royal after Queen Anne, and Acadia was renamed Nova Scotia.

Following his successful role in the capture of Acadia, Nicholson—a general now—returned to England and persuaded Queen Anne to supply him with enough men and ships to complete the conquest of Canada. Queen Anne and her ministers agreed.

In the summer of 1711, there lay anchored in Boston Harbor the largest single expeditionary force that England had ever sent to sea—fifteen men-of-war and more than forty troop transports carrying some 12,000 troops, many of whom were veterans of the fighting in Europe. This expeditionary force was to attack Quebec. In addition, about 2,500 veteran colonial Indian fighters, under the command of General Nicholson, were to spearhead an overland attack against Montreal.

Everything pointed to success for the British and their colonial comrades-in-arms, but once again victory was to elude a two-pronged attack against Quebec and Montreal. In command of the British amphibious operation against Quebec was Admiral Sir Hovenden Walker, and it was Walker who would manage to snatch defeat from the jaws of victory.

Walker was not a good navigator despite his rank of admiral, and he somehow managed to allow ten of his warships to run aground on a series of shoals in the St.

Lawrence River. More than seven hundred men drowned when the ships quickly sank after having their bottoms ripped out by the rocky shoals. Walker, who had earlier admitted he had no taste for a long campaign against Canada, immediately ordered his remaining ships to sail back to England. Walker's bad luck was not yet over, for his flagship blew up in the Thames estuary killing several hundred more men. He was later dismissed from the Royal Navy.

As a result of Admiral Walker's fiasco, General Nicholson was forced to abandon his overland attack on Montreal—but not before taking off his wig, when he got word of Walker's hasty retreat, throwing it on the ground and jumping up and down on it.

Fortunately, the war in Europe had by now run its course, and the Treaty of Utrecht was signed on April 11, 1713, to end both the war there and the extension of it in America. By the terms of the treaty, Hudson's Bay, Newfoundland and Nova Scotia were given to the English. There were two other treaty terms that would have lasting significance. One ceded the Rock of Gibraltar to the British, and the mighty rock would become the symbol of British supremacy for centuries to come. The other term gave Great Britain the right to sell 5,000 slaves a year to Spain's colonies.

The border between Canada and the British colonies was not definitely fixed by the treaty, however, and this would lead to continued disputes over the control of the North American continent.

Six

*King George's
War*

Many wars have been started by men losing their heads; only one war has begun because a man lost an ear. Captain Robert Jenkins was the man responsible for the War of Jenkins's Ear, which gradually merged into the War of the Austrian Succession in Europe and King George's War in America.

It all began one hot summer afternoon in the 1730's when the British merchant ship *Rebecca* was sailing through the West Indies bound for England. The *Rebecca*'s captain, Robert Jenkins, and his crew had recently filled the ship's hold with a valuable cargo of a Central American tree called logwood.

After the trunks of logwood trees were scaled of their bark, the exposed heartwood turned a rich mahogany color. The substance in the tree that caused the heartwood to change color could be extracted from the wood and used to dye cotton and wool cloth as well as silks and even leather. Back home in England, the *Rebecca*'s cargo would be worth its weight in gold when sold to textile manufacturers.

The *Rebecca* had barely started on her homeward journey, however, when several Spanish customs ships approached, fired warning shots across the British merchantman's bow and ordered Captain Jenkins to heave to. Jenkins immediately obeyed, and soon armed Spanish customs officials swarmed aboard.

Jenkins knew that his cargo was lost because the area where he and his crew had obtained the logwood was Spanish-held territory. He nevertheless insisted that the wood had been legally purchased. The Spanish customs officials insisted that the wood had been smuggled aboard.

When the customs officials said they were going to confiscate the cargo, Jenkins and his crew objected strenuously. A hand-to-hand fight followed which was quickly won by the Spaniards. Jenkins and his men were forcibly restrained until the wood could be unloaded. Then, to teach the English smugglers a lasting lesson, one of the Spanish officials took out his cutlass and cut off one of Captain Jenkins's ears.

Months later, having managed to recover from the cruel act, Captain Jenkins sailed his empty ship back to

London. There, before a committee in the House of Commons, Captain Jenkins not only described the atrocity but took out a neatly folded handkerchief and displayed the grisly trophy that the Spanish allowed him to keep.

One of the committee members asked Jenkins what his thoughts were when his ear had been cut off.

"I committed my soul to God," he said, "and my life to my country."

When Jenkins's story was made public, feeling in England ran high against the Spanish. Then emotions cooled and for a time Jenkins was temporarily forgotten. But the Spanish continued to board more and more British ships on the high seas and commit atrocities against British seamen. Feelings again began to run high against the Spanish. Jenkins's noble words at the end of his report to the House of Commons were recalled, and "No seizure and search of British ships!" became something of a war cry.

Finally, in October 1739, Great Britain declared war against Spain. This conflict was naturally called, "The War of Jenkins's Ear." It was a relatively brief affair, but while it was going on, a dispute arose among several European nations regarding who should succeed to the Austrian throne and soon the War of the Austrian Succession had engulfed the continent. In America this latter conflict was called King George's War because King George II was on the British throne.

During the War of Jenkins's Ear, there was brief but bitter fighting in America between the British and Spanish in the recently founded British colony of Georgia. The Spaniards from St. Augustine in Florida landed several thousand troops on St. Simons Island off the coast of Georgia. They intended to use the island as a base from which they could attack and destroy the fledgling colony. But General James E. Oglethorpe, who was one of the wealthy Englishmen who had been granted a charter to found the colony, had been foresighted enough to provide a battalion of Scottish highlanders as well as a number of well-trained local militia for the defense of the settlement.

Georgia had been founded as a haven for the poor, the unemployed and imprisoned debtors as well as for people who were being persecuted in Europe for their religious beliefs. King George, for whom the colony was named, was also shrewd enough to realize that Oglethorpe's settlement, if it prospered, could serve as a bastion of defense not only against the Spanish in Florida but also the French in Louisiana. Thus he had provided arms and ammunition for Oglethorpe's military defenders.

General Oglethorpe and his troops met and quickly defeated the Spaniards at the Battle of Bloody Marsh on St. Simons Island in the fall of 1742. This was the only important colonial battle in North America between Great Britain and Spain.

The theater of operations for the control of the North American continent quickly shifted from the south back to the north when King George's War began in the spring of 1744.

Unfortunately, when England was given Acadia, at the end of Queen Anne's War, the Treaty of Utrecht that ended the war left Cape Breton Island in French hands. Control of Cape Breton, which was several miles east of Acadia, enabled the French also to control the mouth of the Gulf of St. Lawrence. From this vantage point they could prey on New England fishing vessels in the area as well as on the whole of New England itself.

Realizing that Acadia would be of little military value to New England so long as the French controlled Cape Breton, France's Louis XIV ordered Cape Breton's main harbor to be heavily fortified. Later, over a period of twenty-five years, the most powerful fortress in the New World was built there. It was named Louisburg after the French king.

Louisburg was ideally situated for defensive purposes. It was on the tip of a spit of land that formed one arm of Louisburg Harbor. It fronted on the harbor where it was protected by an island on which were placed a number of cannon. Directly across the harbor from Louisburg was another defensive fortification also housing a number of cannon. This was called the Grand Battery.

In 1745, Governor William Shirley of Massachusetts decided to eliminate the French threat to New England by capturing and destroying Louisburg. He requested military aid from England. When this was not forthcoming, Shirley decided that New England would have to accomplish the task unaided.

When Benjamin Franklin heard of Shirley's plan, he

warned him: "Fortified towns are hard nuts to crack, and your teeth are not accustomed to it."

Despite Franklin's wise words of caution, Shirley persisted in his plan. Soon the whole population of Massachusetts was caught up in the crusade against Louisburg. There were religious overtones in the fervor with which the Protestant Puritans of Massachusetts adopted the idea of not only destroying French power but also striking a blow for freedom against the Catholics, whom they both feared and hated.

Although the other colonies were invited to join the crusade, only Connecticut and New Hampshire raised any men. Between them they supplied about 1,000 poorly trained troops, and Rhode Island offered a single ship, a sloop called the *Tartar*. Massachusetts with some 3,500 completely untrained men supplied the bulk of the fighting force, which was placed under the command of William Pepperrell, an amateur soldier who had never been in combat. Governor Shirley appointed Pepperrell a lieutenant general.

Massachusetts also supplied a dozen escort ships and some ninety other vessels to transport the troops to Cape Breton. Fortunately, this ragtag and bobtail New England navy received last minute support from Commodore Peter Warren's Royal Navy squadron. Warren dispatched several British men-of-war from the West Indies to join Pepperrell's fleet, which sailed from Boston late in March, 1745.

The amphibious force, including the British men-of-war, arrived at Louisburg on April 28, 1745. The men-of-war immediately blockaded the port, and General Pepperrell prepared to land his assault force at Flat Point several miles east of the main fortress.

The commandant of Louisburg, the Chevalier Duchambon, immediately dispatched about 200 soldiers under Captain Ralph Morpain to repulse the invaders at Flat Point. The Yankees avoided Flat Point, however, after making a feint at it, and landed instead at Freshwater Cove several miles to the west. Before Captain Morpain could dispatch his troops to repulse the Yankees from their new landing point, the New Englanders had firmly established a beachhead.

A few days later several hundred Yankee troops led by Captain William Vaughan circled around the town until they got behind the French cannon in the Grand Battery. Here they captured a naval supply dump containing barrels of tar which they immediately set on fire. As the smoke from this fire rose skyward in a huge black cloud, the troops defending the Grand Battery assumed they were being attacked by the main body of Yankee troops. Hastily spiking only a few of their cannon, the French fled from the Grand Battery, leaped into their small boats and rowed to the main fort.

When Vaughan's small party entered the Grand Battery, they realized that not only had they captured most of the cannon that were meant to defend Louisburg but, more importantly, almost all of the cannon were in good working order.

To signal the capture of the Grand Battery a teen-aged boy, Billy Tufts, climbed the main flagstaff and fastened his red coat to the top as a substitute for the British flag. A volley of cannon shots from the town greeted this effort, but Billy shinnied back down the flagstaff unharmed. Vaughan immediately signaled to General Pepperrell that the Grand Battery had been captured and he was waiting for reinforcements and "a proper flag." The men of Vaughan's party then went to work repairing the few cannon that had been damaged and turning all of the guns in the battery around so they could be fired into Louisburg. Soon cannon fire from their own guns began to rain down mercilessly on the French forces inside the beleaguered fortress.

Meanwhile, General Pepperrell began unloading his cannon from his transports and moving them toward Louisburg. This proved to be an almost impossible task. Sledges to haul the cannon had to be built from tree trunks. Teams of 200 men wearing leather shoulder harnesses dragged each of the guns on its sledge through a marsh to the rear of Louisburg. One gun slipped from its sledge and simply disappeared into the quicksand-like slime. Nevertheless, the men persisted, and soon a semicircle of Yankee cannon partially surrounded Louisburg.

Day after day the cannonade from the captured guns of the Grand Battery as well as those from General Pepperrell's main force continued to rain down destruction on the French. The interior of the fort was pounded to rubble. Finally, even the stone walls of the fortress began to crumble.

Pepperrell's forces suffered almost as much as the French—from lack of food, sickness and the highly accu-

rate small-arms fire from the French defenders. Pepperrell's forces steadily dwindled until they numbered less than 2,000 men.

Inside the fort, the French held out stubbornly, mainly because they had been told to expect relief from one of their largest warships, the *Vigilant*. The Chevalier Duchambon also knew that the attackers were suffering severely. What he did not know, until it was too late to risk a sortie of his soldiers outside the fort against the Yankees, was that the *Vigilant* had been intercepted by several British men of-war and forced to surrender.

On June 15, Duchambon, at last, received word that the *Vigilant* had been captured. He immediately sued for peace terms. After entering Louisburg, the jubilant General Pepperrell wrote to Governor Shirley: "No town was ever so mauled by cannon shells, and never have any troops fought with greater courage."

When the news of the capture of Louisburg reached Boston, the city and then the whole of New England went wild with joy. In England and on the European continent, the news was received with general disbelief. How could Louisburg, the Gibraltar of the New World, be captured by a body of amateur soldiers led by an amateur general?

By now, however, the war in Europe had nearly run its course and the fall of Louisburg simply hastened the signing of the peace treaty. The Peace of Aix-la-Chapelle was signed in 1748, and its terms were received in Boston with even greater disbelief than the news of the fall of Louisburg had been received in Europe. The reason for the New Englanders' disbelief was that, by one of the terms of the Aix-la-Chapelle treaty, Louisburg had been returned to the French.

The siege and capture of Louisburg was the only major action in King George's War. Actually, the war solved nothing and the Aix-la-Chapelle treaty merely made matters worse between the British and the French in North America. For a few years there was a tenuous peace. Then, once again, war broke out. This time, however, the conflict began in the New World, where it was called the French and Indian War, and gradually spread to the Old World, where it was known as the Seven Years' War.

The French and Indian War was the final and decisive conflict in the series of Colonial Wars in America. When it ended, Great Britain would be in control of the North American continent. Before it ended, however, it would become the most dramatic—and also the most costly in men and materiel—of all the Colonial Wars. Out of its cauldron, tested in the crucible of some of the most savage fighting in the history of warfare, would come many of the leaders who would command the colonial forces against the mother country in the American Revolution.

Part II

Seven

*George
Washington
Goes
to War*

By the time he had reached his late teens, George Washington was a tall, rugged young man, standing "straight as an Indian," as a friend described him, and weighing some 175 pounds. His height of six feet, two inches made him truly a giant of a man for the 18th century when few men were more than five feet, six inches tall. He was also quite handsome—a fact that none of his later portraits made clear—despite a slightly pockmarked face and a rather large nose and a jutting lower jaw. He looked, in fact, like a man born to command—an impression he proved true early in his career.

As a youth, George Washington was serious, industrious and ambitious. He was also a somewhat humorless lad, but perhaps his one major fault was a quick and fiery temper, which he constantly fought to control. He was also a fun-loving young man, fond of dancing, parties and sports of all kinds.

George Washington was born on February 22, 1732, at Wakefield in Westmoreland County, Virginia. He came from an old colonial family. His great grandfather, John Washington, had come to Virginia from England in 1657. It was he who first obtained a large tract of land near what is today Washington, D. C. A part of this tract of land on the Potomac River later became the site of Mount Vernon.

John's grandson, Augustine, married twice. By his first wife, Jane Butler, he had four children—two sons and two daughters. When his wife died, Augustine married Mary Ball, granddaughter of Colonel William Ball who had first settled in Virginia in 1650. Mary's mother and father had died before she was thirteen.

George Washington was the eldest of six children, four sons and two daughters, born to Augustine and Mary Ball Washington.

George Washington's father died when the boy was only eleven. His mother then kept George very close to her, although he never in any sense became a "mama's boy." From a very early age he seemed to be a "man's man," learning a great deal about farming and other kinds of practical outdoor work from his older half brothers, Lawrence and Augustine, and the other men of the community.

Young George worshipped Lawrence, and the feeling was returned. This love and affection lasted all of the two men's lives. Before becoming an expert farmer, Lawrence had been a soldier, and it was probably from him that George first gained his interest in naval and military matters. When George said he wanted to join the navy, however, his mother refused to give her permission despite her son's pleas and Lawrence's insistence.

It was Lawrence and his lovely wife, Anne Fairfax, who established the estate of Mount Vernon, which George would later inherit. For a time George lived with them there. He also spent several years with his other half brother, Augustine, at Wakefield.

Very little is known of George's early schooling, although it was quite irregular. (All of the traditional stories about his throwing a stone or a silver coin across the Rappahanock River, and his cutting down a cherry tree and confessing the deed to his father were pure fabrications—stories made up by Mason L. "Parson" Weems, an early biographer of Washington. Not knowing any of the details of Washington's early years, Weems simply created these tales.)

Washington, as a boy, was probably tutored by his mother, and for several years he studied geography, Latin, the English classics and mathematics with a schoolmaster named Henry Williams at Wakefield. George showed a keen interest in mathematics, including trigonometry. It was probably this interest that led him into becoming a surveyor. By the time he was in his early teens, he could use surveyors' instruments well enough to accurately plot the local farm fields.

It was while he was living with Lawrence that George became acquainted with Lord James Fairfax, a cousin of Lawrence's wife. Lord Fairfax was the owner of five million acres of land in northern Virginia and the Shenandoah Valley. He hired George to help survey this vast tract. The job took more than a year, which proved to be rough and dangerous work for the sixteen-year-old youth.

Young Washington performed his job well, however, despite such discomforts as having to spend raw winter nights "under a thin blanket that was double its own weight in lice and fleas," as he recorded in his diary. When the boy returned from this trial in the wilderness, Lord Fairfax had him appointed official surveyor of Culpeper county.

Washington's new official post kept him more than busy for the next two years. But it was extremely profitable work. For each working day (frequently the weather and his other interests prevented his working) he earned a dubloon, which was worth about $15—handsome pay indeed for a teenager of that era.

Washington used his money to good purpose. Whenever he found a tract of land that looked as if it might be valuable in the future, he purchased it. Within a few years he owned 1,500 acres. It was not a life of all work and no play, however. The young Virginia squire also used a good part of his pay to buy the fashionable clothes of which he was so fond. These he loved to wear at dress balls. He also spent much of his free time in riding horseback, breaking horses, fox hunting and other sports such as wrestling.

It was from this generally carefree life of a young country gentleman that George Washington was suddenly called to duty—a call to duty that he was to hear and heed a good many times during his relatively long life.

In 1752, Lawrence Washington died of tuberculosis. In his will he named George Washington executor and heir to Mount Vernon. But Washington did not become the legal owner of the estate until some years later when Lawrence's widow died. The fact that Washington now controlled such an important estate, plus his early record of success as a surveyor in wilderness territory, brought him to the attention of the Virginia governor, Robert Dinwiddie. Dinwiddie was in great need of a brave, self-sufficient young man to carry out an important mission for the British Crown.

For some time, the French from Canada had been building a string of forts in the Ohio Valley from Lake Ontario to the Ohio River. This was territory claimed by the British, and Dinwiddie wanted to send a messenger to tell the French to leave the area. He had already sent one messenger who had not been heard from again. Governor Dinwiddie now chose George Washington for this dangerous job, appointing him a major in the militia.

Washington and a party of six men, including a scout, an interpreter, and four traders, set out for the Ohio country on October 31, 1753. (The Ohio country at this time included much of what later became Pennsylvania.) It took them two weeks to reach what is now Cumberland, Maryland. Despite the fact that winter had set in, the party pressed on through the trackless wilderness and driving snow. They reached Fort Le Boeuf at what is today Waterford, Pennsylvania, near Lake Erie, in another three weeks.

Here the French commander, a one-eyed veteran named Legardeur de St. Pierre, greeted Washington and his men cordially but firmly.

"Our orders are to take possession of the Ohio Valley," he told Washington, "and that's just what we intend to do."

Eager to get this news back to Governor Dinwiddie, Washington set off on his return trip, accompanied only by his scout and guide, Christopher Gist.

The two men turned their journey into a forced march, sleeping only three or four hours out of every twenty-four—and these were during the day so they could travel, unseen, at night. Even so, they were lucky to return at all. At one point along the way, they were ambushed by Indians, one of whom fired a musket at Washington from only a few yards away in a face-to-face encounter. Fortunately, the Indian's musket misfired. On another occasion, the two men almost drowned when their raft overturned while they were crossing the Allegheny River. They almost froze to death in their wet clothing but finally managed to build a roaring fire and thaw out their clothing and themselves. Finally, they reached Williamsburg in mid-January, 1754, where Washington wrote a detailed report of his futile journey. This report was later published in British newspapers, and the twenty-one year-old Washington suddenly found his name a household word.

Governor Dinwiddie next readied an expedition to take over control of the Ohio Valley for the British Crown. Washington was promoted to lieutenant colonel and put in charge of recruiting troops for this expedition.

Meanwhile, Washington urged Dinwiddie to reinforce a British fortress that he been built at the juncture of the Ohio and Allegheny Rivers (the site of modern Pittsburg). Dinwiddie's response was to send Colonel Washington and two companies of militia to take over the fort. Washington and his 160 men set out in April of 1754. Before they could reach their destination, however, they learned that the French had captured the fort, demolished it and built a much larger one on the same sight. They named it Fort Duquesne after the current governor of Canada, the Marquis de Duquesne.

Washington then built his own defensive stronghold at the site of modern Confluence, Pennsylvania, which he called Fort Necessity. Using Fort Necessity as a base, on May 28, 1754, Washington attacked an advance party of French and Indians moving from Fort Duquesne to Fort Necessity. In the surprise attack, the French commander, Coulon de Jumonville, was killed, as were nine other Frenchmen. Some twenty others were taken prisoner.

Soon afterwards, Washington was promoted to full colonel, and he received major reinforcements. His force now numbered almost 400 men. These were not to prove powerful enough, however, to fend off 700 French and Indians who attacked Washington and his defenders at Fort Necessity on July 3, and, after a short but bitter fight, defeated them. Washington and his men were allowed to return to Virginia, following an honorable surrender, but only after promising that the British would not build another fort in the area for a year.

When he returned to Virginia, Washington wrote his half brother, Augustine, "I have heard the bullets whistle, and believe me there is something charming in the sound." He would have ample opportunity to hear that charming sound again in the near future.

By now the French and Indian War had begun. Actually, it began with Washington's first attack on the French advance party near Fort Necessity and the death of Coulon de Jumonville. A British writer, Sir Horace Walpole later said, "A volley fired by a young Virginian in the backwoods of America set the world on fire." (This was not unlike the single incident that triggered World War I, as explained in another volume in this series, *The United States in World War I*.) A short time after this incident, Washington was accused of assassinating de Jumonville, but this charge was never substantiated.

Embarrassed by this charge of assassination as well as by his defeat at Fort Necessity, Washington was further discouraged when he learned that he had been demoted from colonel to captain. He was told that not only he but all colonial officers had been demoted by orders of the

British war department. Nevertheless, Washington took this demotion as a personal affront and resigned his commission. He retired to Mount Vernon, which he rented from his sister-in-law for 15,000 pounds of tobacco a year.

The war began in earnest, early in 1755, when General Edward Braddock arrived in Virginia from England. He was in command of more than 1,000 British regulars with orders to capture Fort Duquesne. (This force was later supplemented by 1,500 colonial militia, including several hundred valiant "Virginia Blues.") One of Braddock's first acts was to ask Washington to serve as his personal aide in the campaign. He offered Washington the honorary rank of colonel. Washington accepted the offer—but only if he were allowed to serve without rank and pay.

As soon as the expedition got under way in the spring of 1755, Washington was appalled at Braddock's unawareness of the methods of fighting against the Indians. The British general marched his red-coated men into every skirmish and battle as though they were on parade. The Indians—not to mention the French who were by now more than well-schooled in frontier warfare— fought from behind fallen trees, underbrush and anything else that hid them from the British. The end result was inevitable.

The final act in this tragedy—the complete rout of Braddock's army—occurred on July 9, 1755, just a few miles from Fort Duquesne.

The British regulars and their colonial comrades-in-arms had hacked their way for more than a month through the thick and trackless forest, encountering minor ambushes every step of the way. Now they encountered a major ambush in which hundreds of their number were slaughtered. Braddock himself was mortally wounded in this engagement, and Washington had two horses shot out from under him. Afterwards Washington wrote the following vivid account of the battle to his mother:

Honored Mother:

As I doubt not but you have heard of our defeat, and perhaps have it represented in a worse light (if possible) than it deserves, I have taken this earliest opportunity to give you some account of the engagement as it happened, within seven miles of the French fort, on Wednesday, the 9th inst.

We marched on to that place without any considerable loss. . . . When we came there, we were attacked by a . . . large . . . body of French and Indians. Ours consisted of about 1,300 well-armed troops, chiefly of the English soldiers, who were struck with such a panic that they behaved with more cowardice than it is possible to conceive. The officers behaved gallantly in order to encourage their men, for which they suffered greatly, there being near 60 killed and wounded—a large proportion out of the number we had!

The Virginia troops showed a good deal of bravery, and were near all killed; for I believe out of three companies that were there, there are scarce 30 men left alive. . . . In short, the dastardly behavior of those they call regulars exposed all others that were inclined to do their duty to almost certain death; and, at last, in despite of all the efforts of the officers to the contrary, they broke and ran as sheep pursued by dogs; and it was impossible to rally them.

The general was wounded; of which he died three days after. . . . I luckily escaped without a wound, though I had four bullets through my coat, and two horses shot under me. Captains Orme and Morris, two of the general's aides-de-camp, were wounded early in the engagement, which rendered the duty hard upon me, as I was the only person then left to distribute the general's orders.

P.S. We had about 300 men killed and as many, and more, wounded.

After this defeat Washington was almost completely discouraged. In fact he told his half brother Augustine, "I have been on the losing end ever since entering the service."

Nevertheless, he was persuaded by Governor Dinwiddie to accept the permanent full rank of colonel and to take charge of defending Virginia's 350-mile western frontier.

Meanwhile, the French and Indian War had engulfed the entire eastern seaboard of the Northern American continent, and there were other valiant American colonial leaders who were to play key—and eventually victorious—roles.

Eight

*Tragedy
in
Acadia*

After the defeat and death of General Edward Braddock in the summer of 1755, Governor William Shirley of Massachusetts became the commander in chief of the British forces in America. Shirley was experienced and successful in military affairs—it was he who organized the campaign that resulted in the capture of Louisburg from the French in King George's War—but now success deserted him.

Shirley placed himself in personal command of a proposed attack on the French fortress at Niagara on Lake Ontario. Starting in late July, Shirley led 2,400 men from Albany to Oswego. But then, for a variety of reasons, he kept postponing any further advance. He delayed until December when winter storms prevented any military action until spring. Leaving part of his force at Oswego, Shirley ordered the main body of his troops to return to Albany. He himself returned to Boston.

Meanwhile, General William Johnson managed to salvage a token victory on the shores of Lake George in an attack that was originally aimed at the French fortress at Crown Point on Lake Champlain.

Johnson was a legendary figure among the Indians of the Mohawk Valley. He was beloved by the red man because he could not only live as they did, but he also believed in equal rights for all men no matter what their color or social status. Johnson had married the niece of a Mohawk chief, and when she died, he married another Mohawk, Molly Brant. Her brother, Joseph Brant, was destined to be a famous and influential figure in the American Revolution in which he and his warriors fought on the side of the British.

A jovial, red-haired giant of a man, Johnson had succeeded in enlisting the Iroquois on the English side during King George's War after they had refused to take part in Queen Anne's War. After Washington's defeat just prior to the start of the Seven Years' War, however, the Iroquois threatened to join the French in their fight against the British—and the Iroquois were all that stood between the colonies and the Ohio Valley. This time Johnson was only partially successful in pacifying the Iroquois, many of whom went north to join the French.

Now, for his planned attack on Crown Point, Johnson

badly needed Indian support. Consequently, he called a meeting at his home and was gratified when more than 1,000 Indians attended. But when the march toward Crown Point began, only 300 Iroquois joined the war party. The rest of the Indians knew that their brothers would be fighting on the side of the French, and they refused to take part in such a battle.

Unknown to Johnson was another unfortunate fact: On the battlefield where Braddock had been mortally wounded, the French had found papers disclosing the British plan for the attack on Crown Point. Consequently, Johnson's force of some 3,500 New England and New York troops and the 300 Iroquois Indians was intercepted and ambushed by the French at Lake George on September 8, 1755. Despite the fact that Johnson's forces were badly outnumbered in this surprise attack, they managed to defeat the French who were led by Baron Ludwig August Dieskau, a German fighting with the French.

Dieskau was wounded and taken prisoner by Johnson's Iroquois allies. While in captivity, the German general was threatened by the Indians whose chief, Hendrick, had been killed in the battle. Hendrick had also been a close personal friend of Johnson and had agreed to fight by Johnson's side despite the fact that Hendrick was seventy years old and had to be aided by his braves to mount a horse.

"What do they want?" Dieskau asked Johnson when the Indians threatened him.

"What do they want?" Johnson roared. "They want to

kill you and eat you, that's what they want. And I'd like to join them."

Nevertheless, Johnson prevailed upon his Indian friends and allies to spare their captive's life.

Although General Johnson failed to take Crown Point, his victory at Lake George resulted in his being knighted by the British and made a baronet. He and his men remained at Lake George all winter, where they constructed Fort William Henry. Later, Johnson resigned his military commission to take a job as superintendent of Indian Affairs.

Johnson lived until 1774, acquiring a half million acres of land in the Mohawk and Susquehanna valleys. There he founded Johnstown, which he regarded as the capital of his empire. Had Johnson lived until the American Revolution, he probably would have been able to persuade the Iroquois to fight on the side of the colonists.

Governor Shirley, on the other hand, was severely criticized in Great Britain for his lack of success. His failure to take Fort Niagara finally resulted in his being recalled to England in the spring of 1756, where he was court-martialed but found innocent. Later he was appointed governor of the Bahamas.

The only complete success the unfortunate Shirley experienced in the opening year of the French and Indian War was his plan to expel the Acadians from Acadia. And this was an accomplishment of doubtful distinction since Shirley and the British were never forgiven for their cruel act.

From a military standpoint there was perhaps some

excuse for driving the Acadians from their native land. Ever since the end of Queen Anne's War when the British had taken over Acadia, Governor Shirley had feared that the Acadians would encourage a revolt against the English garrison there. Louisburg was, of course, still in French hands, and with support from the Acadians— who completely sympathized with the French cause— attackers from Louisburg could recapture Acadia and thus regain control of the whole of Nova Scotia. When the Acadians were asked to take an oath of allegiance to the British Crown, they refused.

Reacting to this refusal, in the summer of 1755 Governor Shirley ordered 2,500 Massachusetts troops under John Winslow to proceed to Acadia. There Winslow rounded up more than 6,000 Acadians, placed them aboard ships, and deported them to various colonies along the Atlantic seaboard from Maine to Georgia. They were often put ashore without regard to family ties or other close relationships. Eventually, some of the Acadians found their way back to Acadia, but most of them never did. The majority of these tragic 18th-century displaced persons finally settled in Louisiana. And it was on an incident that happened during their settling in Louisiana that Henry Wadsworth Longfellow based his poem, "Evangeline."

According to the Evangeline legend—and at this date it is not known how much of the story is factual and how much is indeed legendary—an Acadian couple who were engaged to be married, Emmeline Labiche (Evangeline) and Louis Arceneaux (Gabriel), were separated when they were deported. Louis finally arrived at what is today the town of St. Martinville in Louisiana. Louis, who thought he would never again see his fiancée, married another girl. Heartbroken when she learned that her lover had married, Emmeline soon died. The people of St. Martinville say that Emmeline, or Evangeline, was buried in their town behind the Catholic church. There is a monument to her there.*

Also in St. Martinville there is a famous tree called the Evangeline Oak. Louis-Gabriel stood near this tree, according to legend, on the day that Emmeline-Evangeline and other exiles first arrived in the town. It was in the shade of this giant oak that Louis, having instantly recognized Emmeline, had to tell her as gently as possible that he had long since given her up as lost and had married another.

It was not Longfellow but Nathaniel Hawthorne who was first told the tragic story of the exiled Acadians by an Episcopal clergyman, Horace L. Conolly, who had heard it from one of his parishioners. Hawthorne could see no literary possibilities in the story, but he repeated it to Longfellow, who was instantly inspired by it. The poem he subsequently wrote differs in many particulars from the legendary story, but it catches the pathos and tragedy symbolic of the exiled Acadians.

While Governor William Shirley would always be remembered for the part he played in the forced exodus

*The descendants of the exiled Acadians are usually called, "Cajuns." The Cajuns, who form the major portion of the population of St. Martinville, are all familiar with the story of their ancestors' exodus from Acadia.

of an entire people from their native land, he would not, unfortunately, be so well remembered for an accomplishment in which he could have taken considerably more pride. This was his organization of a group of unique woodsmen, scouts and Indian fighters known as Captain Robert Rogers's Rangers. The rangers, with their methods of infiltrating and operating independently far inside enemy lines, would eventually change the tactics of not only the American but also the British army—and, for that matter, most of the armies of the world. They first went into action in September, 1755, during General William Johnson's defeat of Baron Dieskau's French forces at Lake George.

Nine

Enter
Captain Rogers
of
the Rangers

Robert Rogers was a New Hampshire man, born and bred. And New Hampshire men were an independent lot —rough, tall, sinewy, self-sufficient—used to acting on their own, taking care of themselves at all times, in all seasons, in all weathers. New Hampshire men were their own men, nobody else's. And Robert Rogers was among the best of the breed.

Robert Rogers was born in the frontier town of Methuen, Massachusetts, on November 7, 1731. His father and mother, James and Mary Rogers, and their three sons had come to Massachusetts shortly before Robert, their fourth son, was born. Later another son and a daughter would be born.

Robert spent his early boyhood on the family farm near Rumford (now Concord), New Hampshire. He had little or no formal schooling, but was tutored by the family. The Bible was his main textbook. He was just thirteen when King George's War began. When Indians goaded on by the French began to attack all of the New England settlements, the Rogers family abandoned their farm and fled to Rumford. There, despite his youth, Robert enlisted in the militia and fought against the marauding red men.

Like Washington, Rogers was more than six feet tall by his late teens. He had also developed a remarkable physique and was more than a match for most men in wrestling or any other trial of physical strength. By the time he was twenty-one, he had a farm of his own, but he did not like farming. What he preferred was to explore the northern wilderness on his own, or with a small party of companions, hunting, trading with the Indians—or fighting against them if the occasion demanded it.

When the French and Indian War broke out, New Hampshire was asked to supply men for William Shirley's campaign against Nova Scotia. Rogers quickly recruited more than fifty men and was made a captain of militia at the age of twenty-three. Almost immediately, he began to prove his worth as a scout—not, however, with the Nova Scotia expedition but with General William Johnson's forces at Lake George, the expedition that had originally been aimed at Crown Point.

Soon after Johnson defeated the French forces under Baron Dieskau at Lake George and settled down there for the winter, Governor Shirley began to insist that Johnson continue his attack on Crown Point. But Johnson's army refused to push on until they had accurate information about the strength of the French and their Indian allies in the vast wilderness of forest between Lake George and Crown Point. Under normal circumstances, Johnson's Mohawk allies would have supplied this intelligence. Now, however, his Mohawks deserted Johnson, telling him that winning the one battle at Lake George was enough of a victory. Johnson told Shirley that without scouts to serve as his "eyes," he could not advance against Crown Point.

At this point Robert Rogers and his men—they were not yet called rangers—were recommended to Johnson. When Rogers was asked if he would undertake a scouting expedition to Crown Point, through wilderness where no white man had traveled without Indian guides, he immediately accepted the challenge.

Setting out with four companions, Rogers carried his scouting efforts up to the walls of Crown Point. He and his men returned to Lake George in less than two weeks, and gave Johnson not only a clear and accurate account of the number of men at Crown Point (some 600 French and half as many Indians), but also a detailed description of the fortress itself. Still not satisfied with Rogers's estimate of the enemy's strength, Johnson sent Rogers out on a second scouting expedition a few days later.

On this second journey, Rogers and his companions

scouted not only Crown Point but also Fort Ticonderoga, a new bastion the French were building between Lake George and Lake Champlain. Here Rogers found several thousand French and Indians.

All that early winter of 1755, Rogers and others were sent out on scouting expeditions. It was only Rogers, however, who completed his missions, often bringing back Indian scalps as trophies. The other scouts sent out by Johnson all panicked as soon as they got a few miles from their main camp and came running back to Fort William Henry at Lake George.

Despite the fact that his reports were not accepted at face value by Johnson, Rogers found himself a hero among the men at Lake George. His taking of Indian scalps in the heart of the enemy country was a bold and fearless gesture they greatly admired.

In the end, Johnson lingered at Lake George through the winter, refusing to attack and refusing to leave. When Shirley finally flatly demanded that Johnson proceed against Crown Point without further delay, Johnson's response was to resign his commission.

In the spring of 1756, before he was recalled to England, Governor Shirley formally rewarded Rogers by appointing him captain of an independent company of rangers whose salary was to be paid from British funds. It wasn't long before Rogers was named major of nine such companies. These unique ranger companies formed the scouting arm of the British army in America. In time, they were to influence every nation's army down to the present day. In World War II, for example, both the British and Americans had ranger companies that performed valiantly in Europe as well as in the China-Burma-India theater of war. (This is told in another book in this series, *The United States in World War II.*) During the Vietnam War, the Green Berets obviously traced their beginnings to Rogers's Rangers.

All ranger organizations, that came after Rogers's intrepid scouts and skirmishers, based their training methods and rules on a set of twenty-eight rules and regulations that Rogers himself set down as part of his original training program. Among the most significant of these regulations were the following:

I. *All Rangers are to be subject to the rules and articles of war; to appear at roll call every evening on their own parade, equipped each with a firelock, sixty rounds of powder and ball, and a hatchet, at which time an officer from each company is to inspect the same, to see they are in order, so as to be ready on any emergency to march at a minute's warning; and before they are dismissed the necessary guards are to be drafted, and scouts for the next day appointed.*

II. *Whenever you are ordered out to the enemy's forts or frontiers for discoveries, if your number be small, march in a single file, keeping at such a distance from each other as to prevent one shot from killing two men, sending one man, or more, forward, and the like on each side, at the distance of twenty yards from the main body, if the ground you march over will admit it, to give the signal to the officer of the approach of an enemy, and of their number.*

III. *If you march over marshes or soft ground, change your position, and march abreast of each other, to prevent the enemy from tracking you (as they would do if you marched in a single file) till you get over such ground, and then resume your former order, and march till it is quite dark before you encamp, which do, if possible, on a piece of ground that may afford your sentries the advantage of seeing or hearing the enemy at some considerable distance, keeping one half of your whole party awake alternately through the night.*

V. *If you have the good fortune to take any prisoners, keep them separate till they are examined, and in your return take a different route from that in which you went out, that you may the better discover any party in your rear, and have an opportunity, if their strength be superior to yours, to alter your course, or disperse, as circumstances may require.*

VII. *If you are obliged to receive the enemy's fire, fall, or squat down, till it is over, then rise and discharge at them. If their main body is equal to yours, extend yourselves occasionally; but if superior, be careful to support and strengthen your flanking parties, to make them equal with theirs, that if possible you may repulse them to their main body, in which case push upon them with the greatest resolution, with equal force in each flank and in the center, observing to keep at a due distance from each other, and advance from tree to tree, with one half of the party before the other ten or twelve yards. If the enemy push upon you, let your front fire and fall down, and then let your rear advance through them and do the like, by which time those who before were in front will be ready to discharge again, and repeat the same alternately, as occasion shall require; by this means you will keep up such a constant fire, that the enemy will not be able easily to break your order, or gain your ground.* *

VIII. *If you oblige the enemy to retreat, be careful, in your pursuit of them, to keep out your flanking parties, and prevent them from gaining eminences, or rising rounds, in which case they would perhaps be able to rally and repulse in their turn.*

IX. *If you are obliged to retreat, let the front of your whole party fire and fall back, till the rear has done the same, making for the best ground you can; by this means you will oblige the enemy to pursue you, if they do it at all, in the face of a constant fire.*

X. *If the enemy is so superior that you are in danger of being surrounded by them, let the whole body disperse, and every one take a different road to the place of rendezvous appointed for that evening, which must every morning be altered and fixed for the evening ensuing, in order to bring the whole party, or as many of them as possible, together, after any separation that may happen in the day; but if you should happen to be actually surrounded, form yourselves into a square, or if in the woods, a circle is best, and, if possible, make a stand till the darkness of the night favors your escape.*

XI. *If your rear is attacked, the main body and flankers must face about to the right or left, as occasion shall require, and form themselves to oppose the enemy, as before directed; and the same method must be observed,*

---

*Modern rapid-fire weapons make much of this advice obsolete, but it is interesting to note Rogers's early awareness of the importance in warfare of fire power.

if attacked in either of your flanks, by which means you will always make a rear of one of your flank-guards.

XII. *If you determine to rally after a retreat, in order to make a fresh stand against the enemy, by all means endeavour to do it on the most rising ground you can come at, which will give you greatly the advantage in point of situation, and enable you to repulse superior numbers.*

XIII. *In general, when pushed upon by the enemy, reserve your file till they approach very near, which will then put them into the greater surprise and consternation, and give you an opportunity of rushing upon them with your hatchets and cutlasses to the better advantage.*

XIV. *When you encamp at night, fix your sentries in such a manner as not to be relieved from the main body till morning, profound secrecy and silence being often of the greatest importance in these cases. Each sentry, therefore, should consist of six men, two of whom must be constantly alert, and when relieved by their fellows, it should be done without noise; and in case those on duty see or hear anything, which alarms them, they are not to speak, but one of them is silently to retreat, and acquaint the commanding officer thereof, that proper dispositions may be made.*

XV. *At the first dawn of day, awake your whole detachment; that being the time when the savages choose to fall upon their enemies, you should by all means be in readiness to receive them.*

XVIII. *When you stop for refreshment, choose some spring or rivulet if you can, and dispose your party so as not to be surprised, posting proper guards and sentries at a due distance, and let a small party waylay the path you came in, lest the enemy should be pursuing.*

XIX.　*If, in your return, you have to cross rivers, avoid the usual fords as much as possible, lest the enemy should have discovered them and be there expecting you.*

XX.　*If you have to pass by lakes, keep at some distance from the edge of the water, lest, in case of an ambuscade, or an attack from the enemy, when in that situation your retreat should be cut off.*

XXI.　*If the enemy pursue your rear, take a circle till you come to your own tracks, and there form an ambush to receive them, and give them the first fire.*

XXII.　*When you return from a scout, and come near our forts, avoid the usual roads, and avenues thereto, lest the enemy should have headed you, and lay in ambush to receive you, when almost exhausted with fatigue.*

Rogers and his rangers were by far the most romantic figures in the war, in Europe as well as in America. Their green-and-brown uniforms of fringed buckskin, their thigh-length leather gaiters set them instantly apart as a dashing, fearless, independent band of warriors unique in warfare up to that time.

The rangers seemed to be men of incredible hardihood and ingenuity. They made countless raids in freezing winter weather. Before this, British generals had simply settled down in winter because the weather hindered their armies' freedom of movement. Rogers and his men not only traveled across the snow on snowshoes, but they even engaged in fights on snowshoes. To move swiftly across the surfaces of frozen lakes or rivers, they donned ice skates.

As can be seen from Rogers's rules and regulations, he favored movement by night. This meant he and his men often went for weeks eating nothing but cold, dried food since no fires could be permitted in the heart of enemy country.

While Rogers's Rangers were frequently criticized for their lack of discipline, it wasn't long before no British general in America would begin a campaign unless he had at least a company of rangers at his command. Rogers and his men fought successfully at Halifax in Nova Scotia in 1757, at Ticonderoga in 1758, at Crown Point in 1759, where they completely destroyed a large war party of St. Francis Indians, and they were in the war's final campaign in the Montreal area in 1760. At the end of the war, Rogers himself was sent to Detroit to receive the surrender of all French forts along the way.

However, between the winter campaigns of 1755–56 and the war's end, there was a considerable amount of grim fighting to be done—much of which Rogers's Rangers played no part in.

By now the French and Indian War had become part of a wider conflict that was known as the Seven Years' War in Europe. Fortunately for the Colonies, at the start of the Seven Years' War there came to power in Great Britain a man who believed that the way to defeat the French was to defeat them first in America. Thus, for the first time in the long series of Colonial Wars, America became the main theater of conflict. The farsighted man responsible for this radical shift in attitude was one of the most remarkable statesmen in English history—William Pitt, or Pitt the Elder as he is usually called, father of what was to become the farflung British Empire.

Ten

*The
Tide Turns*

"I know that I can save the country, and that I alone can."

Those were William Pitt's supremely self-confident words when he took charge of Great Britain's government as secretary of state early in 1757.

England had been faring badly in the Seven Years' War in Europe and in the French and Indian War in North America. Pitt's solution for saving England from a disastrous defeat by France was to seize France's overseas colonies, both in America and in India, rather than face France's enormous army in Europe.

Pitt's policy, under Robert Clive in India, was eventually to result in England's complete control of that continent. Pitt's policy, under several men in America, was to result much more immediately in England's complete control of the North American continent.

Before Pitt came to power, the British had suffered a continued series of reverses in the French and Indian War in America. The French and their Indian allies, under a new commander—the Marquis Louis de Montcalm —captured and destroyed the British fortress and trading post at Oswego. Montcalm also led 7,500 French soldiers and Abnaki Indians from Ticonderoga against Fort William Henry at the foot of Lake George. The result was not only the defeat of the British at Lake George but also a massacre of those who remained after the battle and were taken prisoner. At least fifty colonial soldiers were savagely butchered and scalped after they had surrendered, and another 200 men, women and children from the fort were taken as captives to Canada. Many of them were killed during the journey.

British forces, during this period, were also under a new commander, the Earl of Loudoun. He had little or no respect for the colonial soldiers, and as a result he got very little cooperation in return. One of Pitt's first acts after he came to power in England was to recall Loudoun.

Pitt's strategy for conquering North America called for the capture of three strong points. The first goal was Louisburg, which guarded the mouth of the St. Lawrence River. The second was Fort Ticonderoga, which all colonial commanders regarded as one of the keys to the

American continent. The third was Fort Duquesne, where Braddock had fallen. Fort Duquesne was another key to the continent since it controlled the whole of the Ohio country.

Pitt launched his massive, threefold land and sea offensive almost immediately after he took office. To take Louisburg he appointed a little known but highly regarded colonel, Jeffrey Amherst, promoting him to major general. Amherst's amphibious command consisted of 12,000 soldiers and 12,000 sailors. The latter were under the command of Admiral Edward Boscawen. Amherst's second in command was Brigadier General James Wolfe, who, like Amherst, was relatively unknown. Soon both men would be famous.

Amherst and Wolfe were almost complete opposites. Amherst was forty-one and a career officer. He was quiet, studious, cautious. In fact, he planned his campaigns so long and so well that he had been nicknamed the "Cautious Commander." When he finally struck, however, his blow was usually devastating. Wolfe, on the other hand, was much more bold and dashing. Tall, thin, red-haired, he had been a soldier since he was fourteen. He was now thirty-one. At eighteen he had been a major and at twenty-two was the commander of a regiment. He played no favorites, believing that all promotions should be made on merit. This attitude was thought mad by many privileged members of the British government. In fact the Duke of Newcastle once said as much to Pitt. "Mad, is he?" Pitt said. "Then I wish he would bite some of my other generals."

Against Ticonderoga some 15,000 men were to be led by Major General James Abercromby. Pitt did not have a free hand in naming the commander of this expedition. He would have preferred someone other than Abercromby whose men had nicknamed him, "Aunt Abby." Second in command, however, was Brigadier General George Howe, who was described by his fellow general, James Wolfe, as, "The best soldier in the British Army." Also serving with Abercromby were Captain Robert Rogers and 200 rangers. Howe was the only high-ranking British officer who had ever joined Rogers and his men on scouting expeditions.

The responsibility for the capture of Fort Duquesne Pitt placed in the hands of colonial officers and militia. Included among these colonial officers was George Washington.

Pitt's ambitious and bold plans paid off almost immediately with the capture of Louisburg.

This campaign began in the spring of 1758. Louisburg was now a much stronger fortress than it had been when it was first captured by the New Englanders in 1745. After it had been returned to France in 1748, the French had rebuilt and strengthened the fortifications so that Louisburg could now truly be called the Gibraltar of the New World. In addition, its garrison was made up of several thousand veteran soldiers and Indians. A dozen warships mounting more than 500 guns, and carrying another several thousand men, were anchored in the harbor.

For the British and Colonials, Admiral Boscawen commanded a fleet of twenty-three warships and eighteen frigates plus 120 transports bearing the expedition's 24,000 soldiers and sailors. This fleet sailed from Halifax, Nova Scotia, the last week of May, 1758, and arrived before Louisburg six stormy days later. High seas and strong winds prevented General Wolfe from leading the first assault forces ashore for several more days. When they did land, however, it was at Freshwater Cove, almost the same spot where the New Englanders under William Pepperrell had gone ashore thirteen years before.

Wolfe's landing craft for the amphibious assault were large whaleboats. Boscawen's fleet provided covering fire for the landing, but this fire was all directed at Louisburg fortress itself. Unknown to the British, the French had erected a huge log barricade in front of the fortress, and behind this barricade 2,000 French and Indians lay in wait.

The French and their Indian allies held their fire until the British and their Colonial allies were within point-blank range. Then they fired a series of fusillades that destroyed half of Wolfe's forces. Led by Wolfe in the first boat, however, the surviving British continued to row bravely forward through the bloodied surf. Finally, several of Wolfe's boats made it to shore and the men leaped out and found shelter behind a rise in the beach. From here they began to concentrate a withering fire on the French. Wolfe, carrying nothing but a small cane, his long, red hair flying in the breeze, calmly continued to direct his men's fire.

Once Wolfe had established a beachhead, Amherst

poured men ashore, and soon the French retreated from behind their barricade to the fortress. Amherst then settled down to laying siege to the fort, a long, monotonous and grueling business.

Wolfe quickly grew impatient with the siege. After several weeks of it, he insisted that he and his men be allowed to storm the fort. Amherst would have none of such talk, however, and made Wolfe content himself with directing the fire of the heavy siege guns against the fort's already crumbling stone walls. The guns continued to fire twenty-four hours a day, and soon life inside the bastion became unbearable.

Finally, on July 26, 1758, Amherst's patience paid off and Louisburg surrendered.

Meanwhile, "Aunt Abby" Abercromby and his men were not faring nearly so well in their campaign against Ticonderoga.

When Pitt had placed Abercromby in charge of the Ticonderoga campaign, he had secretly hoped that Abercromby's second in command, General George Howe, would be the real leader. This soon proved to be the case.

Howe was not only a natural leader, but he was also beloved by everyone in the army "from general to drummer boy." Although he was only in his early thirties, he had already gone a long way toward changing the traditional training methods of many of the British soldiers in America.

After studying the art of forest warfare under Robert

Rogers and his rangers, Howe had made his own soldiers adopt many of the rangers's methods and techniques. He had gone so far as to make his men cut their hair short (long hair could be too easily grasped by an enemy in combat), made them wear leggings so their trousers would not get caught in the underbrush, and made them darken the shiny barrels of their guns so that they did not flash in the sunlight. He also made each of his men carry thirty pounds of corn meal. This enabled them to live a month without additional supplies.

Every one of Howe's men, officers as well as privates, could carry no more than one blanket and a bearskin, and all were required to cut off the tails of their coats so they could move quickly through the thick forest. In short, Howe tried to turn his men into rangers virtually overnight. Had he lived and had he been able to train the entire British army in America as he believed it should be trained, the outcome of the American Revolution might very well have been changed. As it was, however, Howe's influence was ended with his death at Ticonderoga.

The Ticonderoga campaign began early on the morning of July 5, 1758, when a combined amphibious force of 16,000 men set sail from the foot of Lake George. Included among this force were 10,000 Colonials, more than 5,000 British regulars, and several hundred members of independent companies. Among the latter was a large force of rangers led by Captain Rogers himself. The entire force landed within a few miles of Fort Ticonderoga on July 6.

Montcalm, the French commander, had used a defensive technique similar to that used at Louisburg. In front of Fort Ticonderoga, he had ordered a log barricade to be built, and behind this barricade the French lay in wait for the attack.

Howe was alerted to this barricade by Captain Rogers. Instead of attacking it from the front, Howe decided to go around it and attack it from the side. He himself decided to lead this flanking operation since it would probably prove to be the key to the whole assault.

Howe and his flanking force plunged into the woods early on the morning of July 6. Unexpectedly, however, they ran into a French scouting party and a mutual exchange of musket fire occurred. At first there were just the dull, desultory sounds of scattered musketry through the woods. Then the solid, more vicious sound of fierce, rapid, concentrated volleys was heard by the troops at Howe's rear. In one of these exchanges, General Howe was killed, shot through the chest.

At once panic set in among the British and Colonial troops. Captain Rogers single-handedly almost succeeded in rallying the men, but as he himself said afterwards, "The fall of Howe produced despair through the entire army. With his death the soul of General Abercromby's army seemed to die."

Nevertheless, goaded on by Rogers, the forces aimed at Ticonderoga did manage to fight on for the next several days. By July 9, the battle had become a virtual stalemate, one that could be decided either way by a bold thrust. Captain Rogers argued violently for a continued attack, but Abercromby had also lost his spirit after Howe's death. Meanwhile, on the French side, General Montcalm prepared to make a strategic withdrawal. He delayed this move until the last moment, however, and on the morning of July 10 was startled to discover that the redcoats and the Colonials had retreated. Ticonderoga, if only temporarily, remained in French hands.

The third phase of William Pitt's campaign, the attack against Fort Duquesne, began in the autumn of 1758.

Brigadier General John Forbes was in command of this expedition, which was made up of 5,000 Colonial soldiers and about 2,000 British redcoats. Forbes's second in command was a Swiss professional soldier, Colonel Henry Bouquet, who had been hired by the British to teach the provincial soldiers European methods of warfare. Fortunately, Colonel George Washington had also been placed in command of the right wing of the British and Colonial forces. It was Washington who personally told both Forbes and Bouquet that European methods of warfare would simply not work in the American wilderness.

When he took over command of the campaign against Duquesne, Forbes was too ill physically to exercise any real authority over the troops. During most of the campaign he was literally carried about on a stretcher. Thus it fell on Bouquet's shoulders to carry out Forbes's plans.

The first of these plans called for cutting a new wagon road through the Alleghenies to Fort Duquesne. Washington immediately objected to this, insisting that the route Braddock had taken—he had also cut a wagon road—would be a better and faster route to follow than any new road could possibly be. Washington said that any delay caused by carving out a new route would result in mass desertion on the part of the Indians who were allies of the British. Nevertheless, Bouquet insisted on this new route, and Washington obediently went about following Bouquet's orders—grumbling considerably as he did so. By September 3, they had moved within forty miles of Fort Duquesne.

Washington's prediction about the impatience of the Indians awaiting a final battle proved to be correct. The only thing was that the Indians allied with the French were the first ones to desert. By the time Washington and his men neared Fort Duquesne, the main defenders left there were the French. Most of their Indian allies had silently disappeared into the surrounding trackless forests. There remained, however, several hundred determined red men who had sworn to take revenge against the British for continuing to take the Indians' lands.

At this point, Colonel Bouquet decided that he needed to know exactly what the French strength was at Fort Duquesne. To gain this intelligence he sent forward Major James Grant with some 800 men to observe the fort and take some prisoners. As they neared Duquesne, Grant and his men were ambushed by a superior number of French and Indians. Grant and 200 of his men were captured. Most of the rest of his party were killed; a few managed to escape and make their way back to Bouquet's headquarters.

Despite this temporary setback, Forbes (through Bouquet and Washington) ordered his troops forward.

The French slowed this advance by frequent counterattacks, and casualties mounted on both sides. It was not until November that Washington and his men were able to blaze a trail that brought them to within sight of Fort Duquesne. When they arrived there, they were startled to see little or no activity. Had the French deserted the fort?

Washington sent word to Forbes about the strange inactivity within and about the fort, and Forbes was brought to the site on a litter carried between two horses. The same night that Forbes arrived, accompanied by Colonel Bouquet, a tremendous explosion occurred within Fort Duquesne. At dawn the next day, the British and Colonial forces moved cautiously forward only to discover that the French had fled. Before they had fled, they had not only destroyed the fort by blowing it up, but the few Indians that had remained had also taken their final vengeance: They erected a series of stakes and on each stake was the severed head of one of Major Grant's detachment that had been taken prisoner earlier.

The fall of Fort Duquesne and the capture of Louisburg proved to be the true turn of the tide in the war between Great Britain and France for the control of North America. Before the final decision was handed down, however, there remained one great last act in the drama to be played. This was the capture of Quebec by James Wolfe. There, on the Plains of Abraham, occurred the final conquest of the French in Canada.

Eleven

The Fall
of
Quebec

Prime Minister Pitt promoted James Wolfe to major general for the attack upon Quebec. Amherst was commander in chief of the British forces in North America, but it would be up to Wolfe to succeed or fail in the assault upon Montcalm's forces inside the Canadian citadel. Wolfe gave no thought to failure.

As he had already proven, Wolfe was born to the army colors. In a very real sense he was a throwback to an earlier age for he believed in battle as the true test of a man. He expected to die in battle while he was still young, but he was also certain that he would die as a victorious hero. His beliefs would prove to be all too fatefully true on the Plains of Abraham. Interestingly, Wolfe himself suspected he would not survive this battle. He even seemed to gain a certain melancholy satisfaction in the foreknowledge of his own death.

Wolfe's amphibious force of 9,000 men—including 400 rangers—sailed from Louisburg on June 5, 1759. Admiral Charles Saunders was commander of the fleet, which consisted of fifty warships and 120 troop transports and supply ships. On June 27, they arrived at the Île d'Orléans in the St. Lawrence River about five miles from Quebec.

Shortly after they landed, Wolfe climbed to a high point on the island where he could gain a clear view of Quebec. What he saw gave him considerable pause, and he had a moment's serious doubt about the successful outcome of his mission. As he later wrote Pitt, "The obstacles are much greater than we had reason to expect or could foresee." Gazing up at the rocky fortress high atop the sheer-faced granite cliff, Wolfe knew at once that the campaign would be neither quick nor easy. And in the back of his mind was the nagging knowledge that he must complete the conquest of Quebec before late fall when the St. Lawrence would be filled with ice.

Quebec was a natural fortress. The face of the cliff that fronted on the St. Lawrence was too steep to scale and thus the bastion was unassailable from the two sides that were visible from where Wolfe stood. The St. Charles River protected the city from the north, and Montcalm had made doubly certain the St. Charles could not be used by an attacking force: He had blockaded the mouth of the St. Charles where it emptied into the St. Lawrence.

The west side of the city was naturally open, but this area had been fortified as far back as Frontenac's time. Since then successive commanders had increased the size and depth of this fortified wall. In front of the wall was a moat. Cannon were mounted to fire north and south along this wall so any men who attempted to scale it would be easily destroyed. The cannon could not be fired to the west, however, across the Plains of Abraham.

As he turned away from gazing at the sight of this awesome fortress, Wolfe said to one of his aides: "That must be the strongest country in the world." Wolfe could not know it, but the French and their Indian allies outnumbered the British and Colonials almost two to one. Montcalm's forces numbered 16,000.

The problem now became one of how to get up onto the Plains of Abraham by attacking from the west, which Wolfe had decided was the weak side. Unknown to Wolfe, the French generals fully agreed with him.

On the night after the English fleet anchored at the Île d'Orléans, the French launched their secret weapon against the attackers. This weapon was a small group of six or seven fire ships—warships that had been filled with tar, pitch and other highly combustible material as well as bombs and grenades. These ships were manned by skeleton crews who were to sail the vessels to within collision distance of the British fleet, set their fire ships ablaze, and then escape in small boats. In this way, the French hoped, the British fleet would be destroyed.

Montcalm had been skeptical of the effectiveness of

the fire ships from the beginning, and his doubts were justified. The French naval officer in charge of the operation set fire to his ship too soon, alerting the British who took to their small boats, and with grappling irons, towed the fire ships toward land where they were stranded. When the fire ships began to explode, they presented a most magnificent fireworks display, but the only casualties were French: A captain and a half dozen sailors who failed to escape in their small boats.

On June 30, Wolfe made a bold move, which was led by Major Rogers and his rangers. Immediately opposite Quebec was a small peninsula called Point Lévis, or Lévi. Wolfe sent Rogers and his men forward to capture this key point of land from which the French fortress could possibly be bombarded into submission. As they were on most missions, Rogers's Rangers were successful on this one. They suffered severe losses, but nevertheless managed to gain and hold enough ground for the mounting of several cannon. As soon as Point Lévis was secured, Wolfe ordered additional cannon forward and soon Quebec was being severely shelled.

In July, however, Wolfe suffered a serious setback when he attempted to take a point on the northern shore of the St. Lawrence near the Montmorency waterfalls. By attacking the north shore, Wolfe hoped to draw some of Montcalm's forces from the fortress of Quebec. Montcalm, however, refused to rise to this bait.

At the point where Wolfe and his men landed, there was a long, low mud flat which provided absolutely no

protection to any invasion forces. Montcalm's men simply waited for Wolfe's forces to land and then proceeded
to shoot them down. The result was a virtual slaughter
in which some 500 Englishmen were killed without the
loss of a single Frenchman. To cap the day's disaster, a
thunderstorm blinded the retreating British so that additional casualties were caused by drowning as Wolfe and
his men took to their boats and escaped to their starting
point.

Wolfe now realized that Montcalm would not be so
foolish as to attempt a foray outside the fortress walls
and risk a defeat in open battle. There was, Wolfe knew,
only one way to engage Montcalm and his men in open
battle and that was, somehow, to get up onto the Plains
of Abraham.

For the first time, Wolfe now consulted with his
senior officers as to how this feat might be accom-
plished. The consensus was that an attempt should be
made to land upriver from Quebec, beyond the
mouth of the St. Lawrence and beyond the Citadel itself. This, of course, would necessitate the English
fleet's sailing upriver beneath the guns of the fortress,
but Wolfe's commanders felt the risk was worth taking. Wolfe agreed.

It was not until early September, however, that the
movement of the fleet carrying the invasion forces actually began. The delay was due to the fact that many of
Wolfe's men were sick. In fact, only about half of his
original 9,000 troops were fit for duty. Wolfe himself was
seriously ill—several of his aides had observed the marks

of scurvy on his gaunt hands and face—but he told the army doctor, "I know you can't cure me. Just patch me up for a few days so I can do my duty and I'll be satisfied."

In mid-September, Wolfe finally ordered the fleet upriver beneath the guns of Quebec. Unknown to his aides, Wolfe had learned of a secret pathway leading upward from the level of the St. Lawrence River to the heights of Quebec. This path began at a point called Anse au Foulon that has since been known as Wolfe's Cove. This pathway may have been disclosed to Wolfe by a French traitor, as has been frequently suggested, but it is just as likely that one of Rogers's Rangers—perhaps even Major Rogers himself—supplied Wolfe with the information. In any event, Wolfe knew that if he could get most of his men to the cove in the dark of night, they could be atop the bluff and on the Plains of Abraham by dawn of the next day.

Wolfe used small boats rather than troop transports to carry his men on the last stages of the journey to Wolfe's Cove. In this way he hoped to avoid detection by Montcalm's gunners on the cliff. The British and Colonials were aided in maintaining the secrecy of their movement by the fact that the French had been expecting several supply ships. Thus, when members of the French night watch became aware of boats moving on the river, they thought they were the supply boats.

Even so Wolfe and his first wave of 2,000 men were challenged several times from the shore as they rowed under the fortress's guns. Fortunately, at least one of the

British spoke French, so when the attackers were challenged he replied, *"Viva la France!"* (Long live France) and *"Vive le roi!"* (Long live the king). The advance wave and another 2,500 men under Admiral Holmes landed at the cove without incident.

As soon as the first men landed, Wolfe led them up the rocky path to the top of the 200-foot cliff. The climb was a difficult one, but they managed to crawl to the top—hanging onto bushes and small trees—without mishap.

The first men to reach the top encountered a small force of French guards who were quickly overcome. A number of shots were fired in this brief skirmish, and Wolfe feared the main garrison might be alerted. He needn't have worried, however. Afterwards it was learned that the French garrison had heard the shots, but as soon as the firing stopped, the French decided there was nothing more to worry about.

Once the guard on top of the cliff had been overcome, the path was open to the rest of Wolfe's forces and they streamed up it, even managing to drag several cannon with them. By eight o'clock on the morning of September 13, 1759, some 4,500 red-coated British troops were lined up in two long rows on the Plains of Abraham.*

When word was brought to Montcalm, he hurried to the Plains and was visibly shocked at what he saw. Without waiting for all of his troops to assemble—a number of his reinforcements were at the village of Beauport

*The name did not come from the Bible but from a man named Abraham Martin who had once owned a part of the plains which he used as farmland.

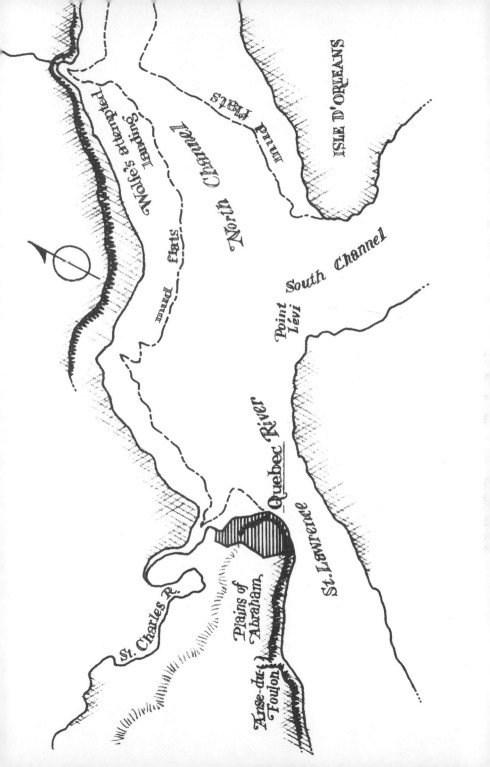

farther down the St. Lawrence—he ordered those who were available to prepare for immediate action. By ten o'clock, 4,500 French—only half of them white-coated regulars—were in battle order facing the British just 500 yards away.

The French moved forward in an uneven line, but their drums beat steadily and their banners swirled in the light breeze. The British stood their ground in grim silence except for the skirl of Highland bagpipes. Wolfe walked up and down the long line of his troops talking quietly to them. Even when the French began to fire at the British from a distance of 150 yards, Wolfe continued his slow, even pacing back and forth despite the fact that he was a clear target.

As the French drew closer, the British continued to hold their fire even though here and there some of their men in the front rank were hit and fell. When this happened, men from the rear rank stepped forward to fill the broken front line. This was the classic European style of fighting, a style that Wolfe and his aides had long admired. Wolfe, in fact, had often told the story of a British army and a French army facing one another on a European battlefield where the British commander announced that he would give the French the honor of firing first.

Today there was no need for such a lordly gesture for the French were firing steadily as they advanced. Wolfe was finally hit on the wrist by a musket ball, but he ignored the wound. On the French came until they were only a hundred yards away, then seventy-five, then sixty

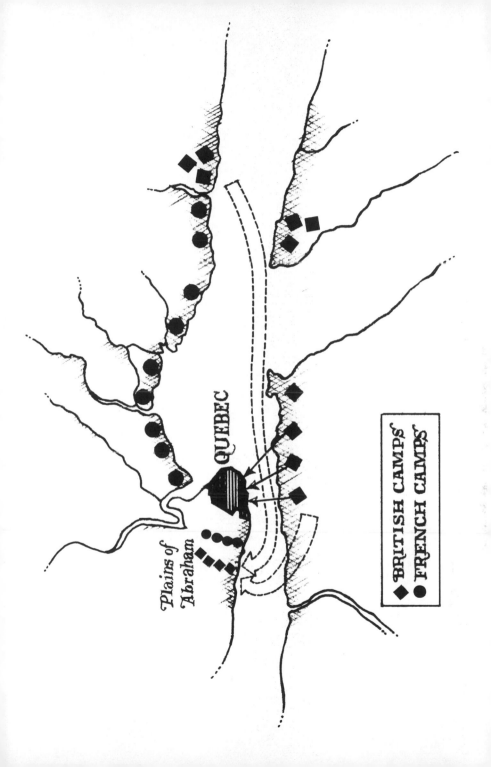

QUEBEC

Plains of
Abraham

BRITISH CAMPS
FRENCH CAMPS

and still the redcoats refused to raise their guns.

At fifty yards Wolfe ordered his men to raise and aim their weapons and at last his voice rang out: "FIRE!"

The first volley took a fearful toll of the French, who hesitated in their advance. Now it was the turn of the British to move forward, reloading their pieces as they did so. When they had advanced fifteen yards, they fired a second volley that shattered the French ranks.

"CHARGE!" came the British command.

Now the British began to run toward the enemy, bayonets fixed and swords at the ready. Panic-stricken, the remnants of Montcalm's command fled back across the Plains of Abraham.

Both commanders were fatally wounded in this brief but deadly encounter, Wolfe during the first British advance and Montcalm during the French retreat.

Wolfe was shot three times in the chest. He was still alive, however, when his men reached his side. When told that the French were in mass retreat and that the British had won a great victory, Wolfe exclaimed, "Thank God, I can die in peace."

Montcalm was carried from the battlefield into a house in Quebec where he died the next day. "I am glad that I shall not live to see the surrender of Quebec," were his last words.

The defeated French were able to hold out within Quebec for a short time, but on September 17, the entire garrison surrendered. After four long Colonial Wars, French Canada had fallen in a few violent moments on the Plains of Abraham.

The French and Indian War did not, of course, end with the British capture of Quebec. General Amherst did not capture Montreal until the following summer. Then he sent Major Robert Rogers and 200 rangers on an expedition to all of the western outposts to lower the French flag and to raise the British colors in victory.

When Rogers arrived at the Great Lakes to take over the surrendered French forts, one of the first people he met was Pontiac, chief of the Ottawas. Rogers was greatly impressed with Pontiac, who stood tall and straight and had a natural air of command. Nevertheless, Rogers was on the alert for trouble since it had been rumored that the famous chief had played a key role in the defeat of Braddock and had otherwise been a thorn in the British side. But Pontiac let Rogers and his rangers pass through Ottawa territory unmolested, hoping that the British treatment of the Indians would be equally generous. His hopes were to be quickly shattered.

Soon after the British took over the forts at Detroit, St. Joseph (now Niles, Michigan), Miami (now Fort Wayne, Indiana) and elsewhere, Pontiac discovered that the British policy toward his people was far more harsh than that of the French. For one thing, the British gave the Indians far fewer presents, including gunpowder which they desperately needed for hunting. The French had always shared their gunpowder with the Indians, but the British rationed it out as small gifts or sold it in minimum amounts.

The French had also always welcomed the Indians inside their forts. The British wanted as little as possible to do with them, inside the forts or outside them. It also became clear to Pontiac that his people's hunting grounds were gradually going to be taken over by the white settlers whose farms began to spread out from the forts.

On February 10, 1763, the Treaty of Paris passed the British Parliament, and both the French and Indian War in America and the Seven Years' War in Europe were officially over. Unfortunately, the conflicts between the white man and the red man that had begun with colonial expansion and were heightened by the rivalry among European nations in their efforts to control America did not end with the Treaty of Paris. Pontiac now knew that the white man's increasing hunger for the red man's land would result in the continuing and growing exploitation of the Indians. He, like King Philip and Opechancanough before him, soon determined to drive the British from his territory.

The best way to accomplish his goal, Pontiac decided, was to unite as many tribes as possible to work together toward a common goal. His first council was held on an island in the Detroit River in April, 1763. Here was formulated what later became known as "The Conspiracy of Pontiac."

Pontiac's plan was to enlist the support of virtually all of the Indians from Lake Superior to the lower Mississippi. In May of 1763, each tribe was to attack the fort nearest to it. Pontiac himself planned to attack Detroit. His attack there, however, was betrayed to the garrison commander, Major Gladwin, and Pontiac was forced to lay siege to the fort. Indians did not like siege warfare, however, and within a few months several of the tribes made peace. Nevertheless, Pontiac's Ottawas held on.

Elsewhere Pontiac's conspiracy was far more successful. Eight of the twelve forts attacked by the Indians were captured. Among the eight that fell were Forts Sandusky, St. Joseph, Miami, Ouiaton (now Lafayette, Indiana), and Michilimackinac.

The latter fort was captured by the Chippewas who approached peacefully and began to play lacrosse outside the stockade. When their lacrosse ball went through an open gate, the Indians followed it inside the walls where they took out concealed weapons and massacred the garrison. Hearing the news, the commander of nearby Fort Edward Augustus, site of today's Green Bay, Wisconsin, abandoned the stockade and fled.

Tribes as far east as Pennsylvania joined Pontiac's war, attacking Fort Pitt, which they failed to take, Forts Venango, Le Boeuf and Presq' Isle, all three of which fell. All of their garrisons were killed and some of them were eaten.

In the autumn of 1763, Sir Jeffrey Amherst from British headquarters in New York sent his aide, Colonel Henry Bouquet, to relieve Fort Pitt. It was here that blankets infected with smallpox were given to the Indians, successfully eliminating them from the war. When Amherst later sent another mission to relieve Detroit, he not only continued to advocate the use of smallpox-infected blankets against the Indians but also recommended the use of dogs to hunt them down. His instructions to Bouquet and the leaders of other relief expeditions in 1764 were to take no prisoners. He also offered a reward of £200 to any man who killed Pontiac.

The Detroit relief party was led by Captain James Dalyell and once again included the intrepid Major Robert Rogers and a company of rangers. (Rogers had returned to New York after originally taking over the surrendered French forts.) Dalyell was killed in the unsuccessful attempt to smash the ring of Pontiac's warriors besieging the fort, but many of Dalyell's men as well as Rogers and his men were able to make their way into the fort as reinforcements. The garrison was also aided by additional men and supplies brought in on a schooner that managed to run the blockade of the Detroit River.

As winter set in and supplies ran low, it became only a matter of time before Pontiac's warriors began to urge him to talk peace. The great Ottawa chief gradually realized that the British were in complete control of the situation. Nevertheless, for another year he attempted to rally other tribes to join him against the British, despite the fact that most of his own Ottawas had now deserted him. Finally, he signed a peace treaty at Oswego, New York, on July 25, 1766. Sir William Johnson signed the treaty for the British.

After he signed the treaty, Pontiac returned to his home on the Maumee River in what is today Ohio. A broken and bewildered man, he lived for only a few years. In 1769, on a visit to Illinois, Pontiac was murdered by an Illinois Indian who had probably been bribed to commit the assassination by an English trader. The assassin's name was Black Dog.

Pontiac's conspiracy formed a watershed between two periods in American history. It ended the period of colonial warfare. Now, ironically, another period of warfare was about to begin in which Pontiac's Indians, who had just finished fighting so bitterly against the British, would be the allies of the British. But as Pontiac could have told them had he lived, no matter which side won, the Indians would be the eventual losers.

There was further irony in the fact that the Treaty of Paris that seemingly had given Great Britain a North American empire was to produce just the opposite result. The British colonists along the eastern seaboard of North America had now had their first taste of independence. True, they had needed Great Britain to help them defeat the French. But now they began to wonder if they still needed Great Britain's authority over them. None of them felt like Englishmen any longer—they felt like Americans. Why then should they continue to bow down to the British?

These growing feelings of independence were to result finally in the colonies throwing off the yoke of Great Britain, but only after yet one more long and extremely difficult war: The American Revolution.

*Suggested
Reading*

The best history of the American Colonial Wars, and for that matter the best history of the entire British and French colonial period in North America, was written by Francis Parkman. Every modern author who has written about this early period is totally indebted to Parkman, as is made clear in all of these historians' footnotes and bibliographies.

Parkman's work, however, is of interest mainly to the advanced student and scholar. Entitled, *France and England in North America,* it runs to nine full volumes, most of which can be found only in large city public libraries. Parkman wrote these books between 1865 and 1892, and they established him as America's premier historian—a position that has not been successfully challenged to this day.

Relatively recently Samuel Eliot Morison, a premier historian in his own right, edited an excellent condensed version of Parkman's monumental work. It is titled *The Parkman Reader.* This is a paperback book published by Little, Brown & Co., Boston, Toronto, 1955.

Probably the best of all of the more recent adult histories of this period is *The Colonial Wars, 1689–1762* by Howard H. Peckham in the Chicago History of American Civilization series edited by Daniel J. Boorstin. This is published by the University of Chicago Press, 1964, in both clothbound and paperback editions.

Dr. Peckham also edited and wrote an introduction to the *Journals of Major Robert Rogers,* reprinted from the original edition of 1765, and published by Corinth Books, New York, 1961.

The best biography of Rogers is *Robert Rogers of the Rangers* by John R. Cuneo, published by the Oxford University Press, New York, 1959. There is, of course, much material about Roberts in *Northwest Passage* by Kenneth Roberts. This best-selling novel is available in paperback from Fawcett Publications, Inc., New York, although it was originally published in numerous hardbound editions by Doubleday, New York, 1936, 1937.

Other sources of interest include the following:

ADLER, MORTIMER J., editor "The Annals of America," Vol. 2, Encyclopædia Britannica, Inc., William Benton, Publisher, Chicago, 1968.

BERKY, ANDREW S., and SHENTON, JAMES P., editors *The Historians' History of the United States,* Vol. I, G. P. Putnam's Sons, New York, 1966.

EDMONDS, WALTER D., *The Musket and the Cross, the Struggle of France and England for North America,* Little, Brown and Co., Boston, Toronto, 1968.

ESPOSITO, VINCENT J., editor *The West Point Atlas of American*

Wars, Vol. I, Frederick A. Praeger Publishers, New York, 1959.

HAMILTON, EDWARD P., *Fort Ticonderoga, Key to a Continent,* Little, Brown & Co., Boston, Toronto, 1964.

LEACH, DOUGLAS EDWARD, *Flintlock and Tomahawk—New England in King Philip's War,* W. W. Norton and Company, Inc., New York, 1958.

LECKIE, ROBERT, *The Wars of America,* Part I, "The Colonial Wars," Harper & Row, Publishers, New York, 1968.

RUSSELL, FRANCIS, *The French and Indian Wars,* American Heritage Publishing Co., Inc., New York, 1962.

TEBBEL, JOHN, *The Compact History of the Indian Wars,* Hawthorn Books, Inc., New York, 1966.

Index